The Casserole Cookbook

The Casserole Cookbook

Jan Oldham

Ω

OMEGA BOOKS

Contents

INTRODUCTION

Everyone thinks we've just discovered casseroles. They're the 'in-thing'. Well, that's all humbug. We've been making them for years without knowing it. All kinds of wonderful mixtures have been concocted on farmhouse wood stoves, but they were always called 'stews'. However, this means the same thing. 'Casserole' is simply a French word meaning stew. In fact, a casserole is simply a pot — a heavy pot, with a tight-fitting lid, which can be used in the oven or on top of the stove.

My definition of a casserole is any food cooked slowly in liquid in a pot with a tight-fitting lid.

All the recipes in this book can be cooked either in the oven or on top of the stove — it makes little difference. If it's cooked on top of the stove you need a very slow heat, low enough to keep the liquid at a gentle simmer, not bubbling like mad. (I find an asbestos mat is handy.) I proved the adaptability of casseroles when I first bought my house and had to exist for 18 months with a single one-pot burner, while waiting for the kitchen to be renovated. Although I had an oven it was miniscule. However, I managed to cope; and what's more I did a lot of entertaining on a grand scale, for up to 24 people. How did I manage this? Any recipe that said 'cook at a moderate temperature' I just adapted and stuck in my huge jam boiler. I'm not saying it was easy, but nobody complained about the food either.

If you're making a top-of-the-stove casserole, you do need to stir the contents a few times during the cooking, because the heat comes directly from the bottom of the pot rather than from all around the dish. I find my bulb baster, which resembles an outsized eye-dropper, a godsend for basting and stirring at the same time.

But you don't even need a stove to cook a casserole: all you need is a power point. These days there are many sorts of utensils designed especially for this job — electric pressure cookers, woks, frypans, saucepans, and Crock-Pots or slow cookers. Everything's gone electric. The idea isn't new, just the energy source. In my mother's day, ordinary pressure cookers were the rage; going back even further, my grandmother used to swear by the merits of straw-box cooking where the food was heated then left in a straw-lined box to cook very slowly (the straw kept it well insulated and so it stayed hot) — both are forms of casserole cooking.

Casserole cooking is simple: easy to make, easy to wash up, easy on the purse and easy for entertaining.

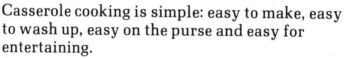

Easy to make? Nothing could be simpler. Just chunks of meat and some chopped vegetables, cooked slowly in liquid for a couple of hours. You don't always need meat; you can use seafood, poultry or vegetables instead. The preparation can vary, but the principle is the same. Sometimes you need to fry the meat first, sometimes you don't. Sometimes there will be a complicated assortment of ingredients, sometimes you use only two or three. Sometimes water is used as the cooking liquid, at other times wine or different liquors are required.

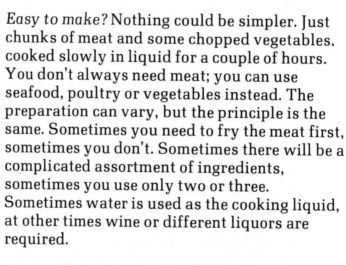

There are no rules for making casseroles. In fact, my recipes need only be suggestions. They can all be varied and adapted, depending on your mood and what you have in the store cupboard or larder.

Easy to wash up? It's obvious: with one-pot cooking, the same pot is used to cook and serve the meal.

Easy for entertaining? Anyone who entertains knows that dishes that can be prepared in advance are a godsend. No last-minute hassle and frantic juggling in the kitchen after the guests have arrived. That's another great bonus of casserole cooking.

Not only *can* casseroles be made the day before, indeed they *should* be. This allows the ingredients time to meld, develop and mellow, giving a rich flavour. The casserole may lack contrast in colour after such slow cooking, but I overcome this by adding additional partly-cooked vegetables and nuts at the last minute before serving.

Easy on the purse? Casseroles use only one pot and one hotplate, thus keeping the fuel bills to a minimum. And in hot, sweltering weather it's cooler for the cook as well. The fewer hotplates burning and the less amount of time spent over the stove the better. With oven-cooked casseroles it's possible to cook more than one dish at the same time. You can cook soup, or potatoes, or a pudding — for the same meal, or for another day — and save on the fuel bills.

With a casserole you do not need expensive cuts of meat — they are wasted. It's not just the expense; the better meats actually don't taste as good as the less expensive cuts. Naturally, a piece of gristly meat is pretty tough, but with long, slow, moist casserole cooking the gristle breaks down into gelatine and melts into the meat, giving extra richness.

Casseroles are generally inexpensive, but you can splurge on the ingredients for a special occasion. Add champagne, liqueurs, truffles, lobster, or avocado with reckless abandon if you wish. All ingredients, no matter how exotic, will complement a casserole. Flick through these pages and you'll see what I mean.

GUIDE TO WEIGHTS & MEASURES

Both metric and imperial weights are given for each recipe in this book; fluid measures are given in cups and spoons as set out below. A good set of scales, a graduated measuring cup and a set of measuring spoons will be most helpful.

Note: For successful cooking use either metric weights and measures **or** imperial weights and measures — do **not** use a mixture of the two.

1 cup = 250 ml = 8 fl oz (an average breakfast cup)
½ cup = 125 ml
¼ cup = 63 ml
1 tablespoon = 20 ml (a generous B.S.I. tablespoon)
1 teaspoon = 5 ml

Weight, volume and liquid measures

In all recipes, imperial equivalents of metric measures are shown in parentheses, e.g. 500 g (1 lb) young beef. Although the metric yield of cup or weighed measures is approximately 10% greater, the proportions remain the same.

Mass (Weight)		Mass (Weight)
½ oz	is replaced by	15 grams (g)
1 oz	..	30 g
2 oz	..	60 g
3 oz	..	90 g
4 oz (¼ lb)	..	125 g
6 oz	..	185 g
8 oz (½ lb)	..	250 g
12 oz (¾ lb)	..	375 g
16 oz (1 lb)	..	500 g (0.5 kg)
24 oz (1½ lb)	..	750 g
32 oz (2 lb)	..	1000 g (1 kg)
3 lb	..	1500 g (1.5 kg)
4 lb	..	2000 g (2 kg)

Liquid Measures	Cup Measures	Liquid Measures
1 fl oz		30 ml
2 fl oz	¼ cup	
3 fl oz		100 ml
4 fl oz (¼ pint US)	½ cup	
5 fl oz (¼ pint imp.)		150 ml
6 fl oz	¾ cup	
8 fl oz (½ pint US)	1 cup	250 ml
10 fl oz (½ pint imp.)	1¼ cups	
12 fl oz	1½ cups	
14 fl oz	1¾ cups	
16 fl oz (1 pint US)	2 cups	500 ml
20 fl oz (1 pint imp.)	2½ cups	

Oven temperature guide

Description of oven	°F	°C	Gas No
very cool	225	110	¼
very cool	250	130	½
cool	275	140	1
slow	300	150	2
moderately slow	325	170	3
moderate	350	180	4
moderately hot	375	190	5
hot	400	200	6
very hot	425	220	7
very hot	450	230	8

These temperatures are meant as a guide only as stoves vary. Follow the manufacturer's guide for your particular oven.

Substitutions

cooking chocolate: 30 g (1 oz)	= 3 tablespoons cocoa + 30 g (1 oz) butter
cream, sour: 1 cup	= 1 tablespoon lemon juice or white vinegar + cream to make 1 cup (*see* sour milk)
garlic, fresh: 1 clove	= ¼ teaspoon powdered or to taste
ginger, fresh green root	= Use preserved ginger with syrup washed off, or ¼-½ teaspoon ground ginger to 1 tablespoon grated fresh ginger root
herbs, fresh chopped: 1 tablespoon	= 1 teaspoon dried or ½ teaspoon powdered
milk, fresh: 1 cup	= ½ cup evaporated milk + ½ cup water
milk, sour: 1 cup	= 1 tablespoon lemon juice or white vinegar + milk to make 1 cup with similar flavour and reaction in cooking. To get the true, thick consistency, warm slightly
self raising flour: 1 cup	= 1 cup plain flour + 2 teaspoons baking powder
yeast, compressed: 30 g (1 oz)	= 2 teaspoons (1 sachet - 7 g or ¼ oz) active dry yeast

Equivalents

Key — t — teaspoon (5 ml)
T — tablespoon (20 ml)
C — 250 ml metric cup in conjunction with metric weight, or 8 fl oz cup in conjunction with imperial weight

Ingredient	30g 1 oz	125g 4 oz	250g 8 oz
almonds, ground	¼C	1¼C	2¼C
slivered	¼C	1C	2¼C
whole	¼C	¾C	1½C
apricots, dried, chopped	¼C	1C	2C
whole	3T	1C	1¾C
arrowroot	2T	⅔C	1⅓C
barley	2T	⅔C	1¼C
breadcrumbs, dry	¼C	1C	2C
soft	½C	2C	4¼C
biscuit crumbs	¼C	1¼C	2¼C
butter, margarine or fat	6t	½C	1C
cheese, grated, lightly packed			
natural Cheddar	¼C	1C	2C
processed Cheddar	2T	¾C	1⅔C
Parmesan, Romano (i.e. hard grating cheese)	¼C	1C	2¼C
cherries, glacé, chopped	2T	¾C	1½C
whole	2T	⅔C	1⅓C
cocoa	¼C	1¼C	2¼C
coconut, desiccated	⅓C	1⅓C	2⅔C
shredded	⅔C	2½C	5C
cornflour, custard powder	3T	1C	2C
cornflakes	1C	4½C	8⅓C
currants	2T	¾C	1⅔C
dates, chopped	2T	¾C	1⅔C
whole, pitted	2T	¾C	1½C
figs, dried, chopped	2T	¾C	1½C
flour, plain or self-raising	¼C	1C	2C
wholemeal	3T	1C	1¾C
fruit, mixed dried	2T	¾C	1½C
haricot beans	2T	⅔C	1¼C
milk powder, full cream	¼C	1¼C	2¼C
non-fat	⅓C	1½C	3¼C
nuts *see under names*			
oatmeal	2T	¾C	1⅔C
pasta, short (e.g. macaroni)	2T	¾C	1⅔C

Ingredient	30g 1 oz	125g 4 oz	250g 8 oz
peanuts, shelled, raw, whole	2T	¾C	1½C
roasted, whole	2T	¾C	1⅔C
chopped	¼C	1C	2C
peas, split	2T	⅔C	1¼C
peel, mixed	2T	¾C	1½C
prunes, whole, pitted	2T	¾C	1¼C
raisins	¼C	¾C	1½C
rice, short grain, raw	2T	⅔C	1¼C
long grain, raw	2T	¾C	1½C
rolled oats	2T	1⅓C	2¾C
semolina	2T	¾C	1½C
sugar, white crystalline	6t	½C	1C
caster	5t	½C	1¼C
icing	2T	¾C	1½C
brown, firmly packed	2T	¾C	1½C
sultanas	2T	¾C	1½C
walnuts, chopped	¼C	1C	2C
halved	⅓C	1¼C	2½C
yeast, active dried	8t	—	—
compressed	6t	—	—

Getting into gear

My ideal casserole dish is one that looks
fabulous and cooks brilliantly — ideally these
two aspects should always go together. When
there are so many types of casseroles available
it's very hard to decide what sort to choose, and
I can never resist buying yet another to add to
my bulging collection. Here's my list of the
many different types of casseroles available to
help you decide which sort to buy.

1

2

3

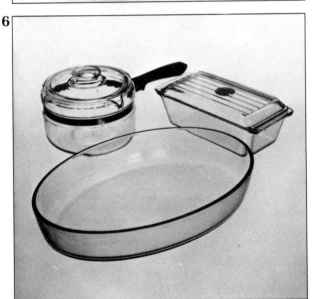

1 My most-used casserole is a large, brownish-black, hotplate-to-table dish. I can use it as a saucepan, a casserole dish and a serving dish. I think this versatility is real value for money.

2 Some casseroles can be used in the freezer, at the stove and on the table. They are sold with extra plastic tops to seal them in the freezer. They're beaut because you can cook, freeze, thaw, reheat and serve all in the same container.

3 Ovenproof earthenware casseroles are only suitable for oven cooking and serving on the table. But who can resist a couple of beautiful hand-thrown pots on the dresser?

4 Cast-iron casseroles are great for top of the stove and oven to table cooking. They might be heavy, but the weight also means superb even cooking. Some cast-iron casseroles have an enamel coating. They come in many bright colours. They are all suitable for use on the hotplate, in the oven and on the table. I find the food tends to catch and burn occasionally, but because enamel is easy to clean, this doesn't really matter. Some have a non-stick inside surface. Enamel dishes are also useful for day-long marinading unlike aluminium, which can be discoloured by long soaking, and some clay pots, which absorb flavours.

5 Stainless steel is easy to clean and comes in a great variety of qualities and sizes. It's great for those health freaks among us; however, I find the steel does tend to burn easily.

6 Special ovenproof glass casseroles are great because you can see what's going on inside. They are super for layered casseroles such as moussaka because you can see the beautifully coloured layers. Some brands need an asbestos mat or wire under them for direct hotplate cooking, but these are usually provided by the manufacturer.

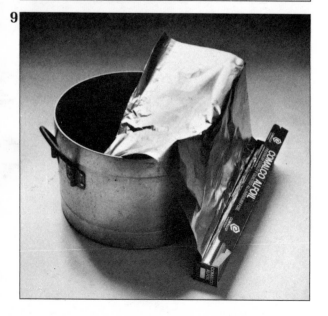

7 Copper looks superb, but it needs to be tin-lined to be suitable for cooking food. It's still the best metal there is for heating evenly. This is why stainless steel dishes usually have a copper base. Copper pans are very beautiful, but need tender, loving care to keep them burnished and glowing.

8 Lovely aluminium pans for waterless cooking are also available. Plain aluminium produces very even, non-burning heat, but can pit and stain with some foods. I usually overcome this problem by using aluminium saucepans with a non-stick surface on the inside. My favourite pans — those I use all the time — are manufactured by Harding and Wood.

9 Another point is that any ovenproof dish or saucepan can be used as a casserole. I use my jam boiler for casseroles. It doesn't have a lid, but it's great for huge quantities, so I fashion a makeshift lid with aluminium foil. Be inventive: you don't need to buy special dishes to cook successful casseroles.

Remember, if the casserole is going straight from stove to table, it's *hot*. So don't burn the table by plonking it straight down.

A collection of casserole dishes

Something to beef about

Ask anyone for their favourite casserole and it's an odds-on bet a beef dish is the winner — whether it be stew, oxtail, curry, goulash, stroganoff or bourgnignonne.

However, the age of being able to afford rump and fillet every day of the week is gone. With inflation and rising prices beef is becoming a luxury. But with casseroles you can still afford to keep it on your menu. Expensive cuts of meat are wasted in a casserole, they don't taste as good as inexpensive cuts, such as stewing steak. The more muscle in the meat, the more flavour it has. Naturally, muscle is tough, so it needs moist, long cooking to break down the gristle and tissue to fork-cutting tenderness.

All inexpensive cuts of beef need slow cooking, whether it is skirt, chuck, blade, topside, or brisket. These economical cuts help keep things on an even keel when you're forced to watch the pennies.

If you are budgeting and/or bulk-buying, you will often have up to half a bullock packaged in the freezer. And this is where casseroles are such a godsend, for they can transform the same cuts of beef into many totally different dishes.

Beef n' Beans (page 22)

A BASIC MEAT CASSEROLE

1 Buy the meat in thick slices for easy handling. Trim off all the fat, but don't trim off the gristle marbling the meat — it melts into the meat and moistens it during the long, slow cooking. Trim off any thick sinews. Cut the meat into large square chunks, remembering that meat shrinks during cooking and you want to end up with each piece a decent mouthful.

2 Toss meat chunks in flour seasoned with salt, pepper, herbs or other dry flavourings, such as packet mixes. Either use a plate to hold the seasoned flour, or shake the meat with the flour in a paper or plastic bag.

3 Fry the meat until well browned on all sides in butter, margarine, dripping or oil. Sometimes a mixture of butter and oil is used; the butter for flavouring and the oil to allow the butter to reach a high temperature without burning.

Only cook a handful of meat at a time. If the meat is added all at once it can lower the temperature of the oil so that the meat just stews and won't brown well. When meat is brown remove it and fry any vegetables used. Return meat to the pan when vegetables are slightly browned and softened.

4 Remove the pot from the stove and add the liquid all at once. Stir until well combined and all lumps have gone. This addition off the heat means you don't get a lumpy sauce. Return pot to the heat and bring to the boil, stirring up the crusty pan scrapings. Then either top with a lid and simmer until the meat is tender, or tip the contents into a casserole dish and bake in the oven until tender.

SAVOURY STEW

Serves: 4

2 tablespoons butter or margarine
3 onions, sliced
750 g (1½ lb) blade or stewing steak
1 teaspoon salt
1 teaspoon sugar
1 teaspoon bicarbonate of soda
2 tablespoons plain flour
2 cups water
3 tablespoons tomato ketchup
1 teaspoon Worcestershire sauce
2 tablespoons plum jam

Melt the butter in a saucepan and fry the onion until tender and lightly browned. Remove fat and cut the meat, into small chunks, add to the saucepan and brown quickly. Mix the salt, sugar, bicarbonate of soda and flour to a paste with a little of the cold water. Stir the sauces and the remaining water into this mixture and pour over the meat and onions. Cover the saucepan and simmer for 2½-3 hours, until the meat is tender.

Note: Savoury Stew may also be cooked in a lidded casserole dish in a moderately slow oven for 2½-3 hours or until tender.

BEEF SPAGHETTI SPECIAL

Serves: 3-4

500 g (1 lb) stewing steak, cut into
   chunks
1 tablespoon oil
1 x 865 g (28 oz) can stockpot soup
   or 2 medium cans beef and
   vegetable soup
2 medium carrots, diced into chunks
1 large onion, chopped
1 cup frozen beans or peas
1 large tomato, sliced
salt
Worcestershire sauce to taste
½ cup water
serving of cooked spaghetti
chopped parsley

Brown steak in oil till well seared. Add stockpot soup. Simmer gently for 15 minutes. Add carrots, onion, beans, tomato, salt and Worcestershire sauce and water. Cover with lid and simmer for 1 hour or until tender. If mixture becomes too dry, extra water may have to be added. Serve with spaghetti piled around meat mixture in the centre of serving dish. Sprinkle chopped parsley as garnish. Serve immediately.

Note: Beef Spaghetti Special may also be cooked in a lidded casserole dish in a moderately slow oven for 1½-2 hours or until tender.

SIMPLE BEEF STEW

Serves: 4

1 kg (2 lb) stewing steak
1 tablespoon butter or margarine
4 lamb kidneys
2½ cups white wine
1 small turnip, sliced
1 swede, sliced
2 carrots, sliced
1 heaped teaspoon mixed herbs
salt and pepper
3 onions, chopped
1 small green pepper, sliced

Remove fat and cut beef into bite-sized pieces. Place in a heavy saucepan over a low heat and fry in butter or margarine. When browned all over, add kidneys and white wine. Allow to simmer 30 minutes. Add turnip, swede and carrots and allow to cook a further 30 minutes. Add herbs, season with salt and pepper and add onions and green pepper. Simmer until onions are cooked but still crunchy.

Note: Simple Beef Stew may also be cooked in a lidded casserole dish in a moderately slow oven for 1-1½ hours or until tender, and this stew improves with reheating.

BEEF N' BEANS

Serves: 4-6

500 g (1 lb) red kidney beans
4-8 rashers bacon, chopped
1 kg (2 lb) chuck or stewing steak, cut
    into chunks
2 onions, sliced
¼ cup tomato paste
1-2 cloves garlic, crushed
1 x 425 g (15 oz) can tomatoes
1 bouquet garni (see page 82)
2 tablespoons brown sugar
4 beef stock cubes
salt and pepper
thyme or mixed herbs
water to cover

Soak beans in water overnight. Fry bacon until fat begins to run. Add meat and fry till well browned. Remove meat and put aside. Add onions to pan and fry till soft. Return meat to pan with all other ingredients. Pour in enough water to cover well. Top with a lid and simmer gently for 2½-3 hours, or till beans are soft and cooked. If casserole looks too dry add a.little more water.

This recipe can also be cooked in a pressure cooker. Simmer under pressure for about 1 hour. The beans may be used without the overnight soaking, but they will tend to break up.

Variation: If preferred, 4-6 cups drained, canned kidney beans may be used. Cook the beef and other ingredients, with about 1-2 cups liquid, till tender, then add canned beans and reheat for 10-15 minutes.

Note: Beef n' Beans may also be cooked in a lidded casserole dish in a moderate oven for 2½-3 hours or until tender.

CURRIED STEAK

Serves: 4-6

1 kg (2 lb) chuck or stewing steak
walnut-sized piece root ginger
1 large cooking apple
2 tablespoons oil
1 large onion, chopped
1 clove garlic, crushed (optional)
1 cup sliced celery
1 cup sliced carrot
1 tablespoon brown sugar
1 tablespoon curry powder
2 teaspoons salt
¼ teaspoon pepper
1 cup beef stock (see page 154) or water
    and beef stock cube
1 tablespoon lemon juice
finely grated rind of 1 lemon
3 cloves
½-1 cup sultanas or raisins
2 tablespoons cornflour

Cut meat into small, bite-size cubes. Chop ginger finely. Peel, core and chop apple. Heat oil in a large saucepan, and add prepared ginger, apple and other vegetables and sugar. Fry until browned. Add curry powder, salt and pepper, fry a few minutes more, then add prepared meat, stock, lemon juice, rind and cloves. Cover and bring to boiling point. Reduce heat and simmer gently for 2 hours. Add washed sultanas or raisins and continue to cook slowly until meat is tender — about 30 minutes longer. Taste and adjust flavourings.

Blend cornflour to a smooth paste with a little cold water, add to curry, stir gently until thickened. Serve curry with boiled rice.

Note: Curried Steak can also be cooked in a lidded casserole dish in a moderately slow oven for 1½-2 hours or until tender.

STEAK WITH PRUNES

Serves: 4-6
Oven temperature: moderately slow

1 kg (2 lb) chuck or stewing steak
2 tablespoons plain flour
2 teaspoons salt
freshly ground pepper
1 tablespoon brown sugar
250 g (8 oz) prunes
1 large onion, finely chopped
2 teaspoons soy sauce
1 tablespoon vinegar
1 tablespoon fruit chutney
¾ cup water

Cut steak into small chunks. Mix the flour, salt, pepper and sugar in a clean paper bag. Add meat, shake together until coated. Stone prunes. Place layers of meat, onions and prunes in a casserole finishing with a layer of meat. Mix soy sauce, vinegar, chutney and water; pour over contents of casserole. Cover with a piece of aluminium foil, then the lid. Bake in a moderately slow oven for 2 hours, or until cooked.

BEEF RAGOÛT WITH CELERY AND WALNUTS

Serves: 4-6
Oven temperature: moderate

750 g (1½ lb) stewing steak
1 tablespoon each of oil and butter or
    margarine
12 button onions
½ tablespoon plain flour
½ cup red wine
1 clove garlic, crushed
1 x 865 g (28 oz) can stockpot soup or
    2 medium cans beef and vegetable
    soup
6 sticks celery
1 tablespoon butter or margarine
pinch salt
1-2 tablespoons shelled walnuts

Cut steak into small chunks and brown in oil and butter or margarine in a thick casserole. Add peeled onions. Stir in flour and cook for a minute, then add red wine, and garlic. Pour soup over meat and vegetables, cover with a lid and cook in moderate oven for 1½-2 hours or until the meat is tender. Slice the celery. Heat butter or margarine in frying pan; fry celery and walnuts with a pinch of salt. When casserole is ready to serve, garnish with celery and walnuts.

MIKE WALSH SPECIAL

Serves: 4-6
Oven temperature: slow

1 kg (2 lb) lean beef
2 tablespoons olive oil
1 onion, chopped
1 teaspoon mustard powder
3 tomatoes
1 large courgette, chopped
1 carrot, chopped
1 clove garlic, crushed
3 rashers bacon, trimmed and chopped
1 teaspoon freshly chopped thyme or
    rosemary
½ cup water or white wine (optional)
salt and pepper

Trim the meat, removing all fat and gristle. Cut into large pieces. Heat oil in a large saucepan. Add meat and fry until well browned. Add onion and mustard powder. Fry until onion begins to soften. Add all other ingredients, including the water or wine if necessary. (There is usually enough liquid from the vegetables.) Top with a very tight lid. Cook very slowly in a slow oven for 2-3 hours or until tender.

OLIVE BEEF STOCK POT

Serves: 3-4
Oven temperature: moderate

750 g (1½ lb) topside or stewing steak,
  cut into chunks
1-2 tablespoons plain flour
salt and pepper
1 tablespoon fat, butter or margarine
1 green pepper, sliced
2 onions, sliced
6 stuffed olives, sliced
1 tablespoon olive juice
1 x 865 g (28 oz) can stockpot soup or
  2 medium cans beef and vegetable
  soup
1 tablespoon tomato paste
1 teaspoon sugar
1 cup water

Rub steak with flour, salt and pepper, and brown in hot fat, butter or margarine in pan. Place browned steak in casserole dish and top with sliced pepper, onions and olives. Mix olive juice, can of stockpot soup, tomato paste and sugar, and pour over meat, adding water. Put lid on casserole and bake in moderate oven approximately 1½ hours. Serve with boiled rice.

SPICY BEEF

Serves: 4-6

1 kg (2 lb) topside or stewing steak
1 cup port wine
2 teaspoons powdered ginger
plain flour
salt and pepper
oil
1 cup beef stock (see page 154) or water
  and stock cubes, or 1 cup canned beef
  consommé
juice of 1 lemon
1 cup mandarin segments, fresh or
  canned

Slice the steak thinly and soak in port wine and ginger for 2-2½ hours. Strain the meat and reserve the liquor. Toss the meat lightly in flour, salt and pepper. Fry in heated oil until well browned, cooking a few pieces at a time. Add the beef stock and reserved marinade. Top with a lid and simmer over a low heat for 1-1½ hours or until meat is tender. Add the lemon juice, mandarin segments and season with pepper and salt shortly before serving. This is best served with fluffy mashed potatoes.

Note: Spicy Beef may also be cooked in a lidded casserole dish in a moderately slow oven for 1½-2 hours or until tender.

JON'S EASY CASSEROLE

Serves: 4-6

1 kg (2 lb) stewing steak
4 tablespoons plain flour
salt and pepper
2-3 tablespoons oil
1 cup burgundy or dry red wine
2 cups pineapple pieces, or 1 medium can

Trim the meat well, removing gristle and and cut into cubes. Mix flour, salt and pepper and roll meat in it to coat. Fry in hot oil until well browned. Add burgundy or red wine and pineapple pieces with half of the tinned syrup. Cover and cook gently for about 1 hour or until tender.

This recipe can be frozen and stored for future use. To serve after freezing, thaw, then reheat, adding an extra ½ cup of red wine.

Note: Jon's Easy Casserole may also be cooked in a lidded casserole dish in a moderately slow oven for 1½-2 hours.

BURGUNDY BEEF

Serves: 6-8
Oven temperature: moderate

1 tablespoon olive oil
1 kg (2 lb) lean beef, cut into 2.5 cm (1 inch) cubes
1 slightly rounded tablespoon plain flour
1 teaspoon salt
¼ teaspoon pepper
1 cup burgundy or red wine
1 cup beef stock (see page 154) or water and stock cubes
1 clove garlic, crushed
1 bay leaf
½ teaspoon dry thyme
4 sprigs parsley
6 baby carrots, peeled
3 small parsnips, peeled
500 g (1 lb) green peas, cooked

Heat oil in pan and quickly brown beef on all sides. Lift beef out into a casserole dish. Sprinkle flour into oil remaining in pan; add salt and pepper. Stir until smooth, then cook until flour browns. Remove from heat, add the burgundy, stock, crushed garlic, bay leaf, thyme and parsley. Combine, then bring to the boil and cook until thickened. Pour over steak in casserole. Cover and cook in a moderate oven for 1½ hours, or until the meat is almost tender. Meanwhile, prepare vegetables, cutting the carrots and parsnips into uniform-sized pieces. Add to the casserole and bake a further 40 minutes. Just before serving add the cooked peas.

BEEF STROGANOFF

Serves: 4-6

1 kg (2 lb) lean steak
4 tablespoons butter or margarine
1 tablespoon seasoned flour
1½ cups thinly sliced mushrooms
1 cup finely chopped onion or shallots
2 small cloves garlic, crushed
3 tablespoons plain flour
2 cups stock (see page 154) or water and stock cubes
1 tablespoon tomato paste
½ cup cream
3 tablespoons sherry

Cut steak into thin slivers. Melt 2 tablespoons of the butter or margarine in a pan. Toss the meat in the seasoned flour, then fry lightly until browned on both sides. Remove the meat from the pan and add the mushrooms, onion or shallot, and garlic and cook, stirring well, for 3 or 4 minutes, or until the onion is barely softened. Remove from the pan. Melt the remaining fat in the pan and stir in the 3 tablespoons of flour. Stir until smooth. Remove from heat, add the stock and tomato paste, and stir until combined. Bring to the boil and simmer a few minutes or until thickened. Return the meat and mushroom mixture to the sauce, cover and cook until the meat is tender — about 1 hour. Just before serving stir in the cream and sherry. Heat thoroughly, but do not allow to boil. This goes well served with freshly cooked buttered rice mixed with chopped parsley.

Note: Beef Stroganoff may also be cooked in a lidded casserole in a moderately slow oven for 1½-2 hours, or until tender.

BEEF CASSEROLE MADEIRA

Serves: 6-8
Oven temperature: moderate

1.5 kg (3 lb) round steak or topside
1 tablespoon butter or margarine
1 tablespoon oil
½ cup chopped carrots
250 g (8 oz) courgettes, sliced
½ cup chopped celery
½ cup chopped onions
½ cup diced ham
3 tablespoons Madeira, port or sherry
1 bay leaf
1 tablespoon brandy
pinch allspice
½ teaspoon thyme
125 g (4 oz) mushrooms
1 cup white wine
salt and pepper
½-1 tablespoon cornflour or arrowroot

Cut steak into cubes. Fry in melted butter and oil until brown. Cook a little steak at a time. Remove meat as it cooks. Fry carrot, courgettes, celery, onions and ham in the same pan until softened but not brown. Add Madeira, port or sherry and boil rapidly until almost absorbed by the vegetables. Add bay leaf, brandy, allspice, thyme and mushrooms. Mix the meat, vegetables and white wine in a casserole dish. Season to taste. Cover and cook in a moderate oven for 1-1½ hours, or until tender.

Thicken with cornflour or arrowroot mixed to a thin cream with cold water. Add some of the hot sauce to this cream, then add enough of this mixture to the casserole to thicken to desired degree. Simmer again for a minute to cook the flour. This recipe can also be cooked in an electric frypan for ¾-1 hour.

Note: Beef Casserole Madeira can also be made with a whole piece of Scotch fillet. Tie meat into a neat parcel with white string. Fry in the butter and oil until brown on all sides. Place on a bed of the vegetables, cover and cook in a moderate oven for 45-55 minutes, or until tender.

BEEF BOURGUIGNONNE

Serves: 6
Oven temperature: moderately slow

1 kg (2 lb) stewing beef, chuck, blade or
**   shin**
4 tablespoons lard or dripping
2 tablespoons plain flour
1 tablespoon tomato paste
2 cloves garlic, crushed
2 cups burgundy
2½ cups beef stock (see page 154) or
**   water and beef stock cubes**
salt and pepper
bouquet garni (see page 82)
60 g (2 oz) pickled pork or bacon, diced
12 button onions
12 button mushrooms
chopped parsley for garnish
2 tablespoons brandy (optional)

Cut meat into large cubes. Fry cubes till browned in lard or dripping in a flameproof casserole. Sprinkle with flour and cook for 5 minutes. Add tomato paste and garlic and cook a further few minutes. Add burgundy and stock, season lightly with salt and pepper and add bouquet garni. Fry pickled pork or bacon lightly, add onions and cook over a moderate heat until they are evenly browned. Add to the casserole. Cover and cook in a moderately slow oven for 2½-3 hours or until tender. Approximately 15 minutes before cooking is finished add mushrooms. Adjust seasoning if necessary and serve hot, sprinkled with chopped parsley.

Note: Two tablespoons brandy are added in the final stage of cooking in traditional Beef Bourguignonne recipes.

CARBONNADE À LA FLAMANDE

Serves: 4-6

plain flour
salt and pepper
1 kg (2 lb) chuck or stewing steak
2 tablespoons oil
6 onions, sliced
1 clove garlic, finely chopped
1 cup beer
1 tablespoon chopped parsley
1 bay leaf
¼ teaspoon thyme

Season flour with salt and freshly ground black pepper. Cut steak into bite-size cubes and coat with the seasoned flour. Heat oil in a heavy saucepan or fireproof casserole, add onions and garlic and cook until tender, but not brown. Remove onions and garlic and reserve. Dust excess flour from meat before adding to pan, and brown well on all sides, adding a little more oil if necessary. Return onions and garlic to the pan and add remaining ingredients. Cover and cook over low heat until meat is tender, about 1¼ hours. Serve hot. Boiled potatoes are a good accompaniment.

Variation: Carbonnade may also be finished with rounds of crusty French bread spread with French or German mustard. Push rounds below the surface of the carbonnade to soak with gravy, and bake uncovered for the last 15-20 minutes of cooking time.

Note: Carbonnade à la Flamande can also be cooked in a lidded casserole dish for 1½-2 hours in a moderately slow oven.

BEEF OLIVES

Serves: 4
Oven temperature: slow

Stuffing
3 tablespoons white breadcrumbs
1 teaspoon chopped parsley
pinch of thyme
½ egg
2 tablespoons margarine
2 tablespoons finely chopped, cooked
   onion
salt and pepper

Beef
500 g (1 lb) chuck steak, in a single piece
2 tablespoons dripping
2 carrots, chopped
2 onions, chopped
2 tablespoons plain flour
1 tablespoon tomato paste
3 cups beef stock (see page 154) or water
   and beef stock cubes
salt and pepper
bouquet garni (see page 82)

To make stuffing: Mix all ingredients together.

To prepare Beef Olives: Cut meat into thin slices across the grain, flatten with a meat mallet until very thin, and cut into 10 cm (4 inch) squares. (Chop any left-over meat trimmings finely and add to stuffing). Spread stuffing on squares of meat, roll up neatly and tie with string. Melt dripping in a heavy saucepan and fry meat rolls until lightly browned. Add carrot and onion, cook until golden. Place meat and vegetables in an ovenproof casserole. Stir flour into fat in saucepan and cook over a low heat for 1 minute. Add tomato paste, cook for 3 minutes. Add stock and bring to the boil stirring continuously. Add salt and pepper to taste and pour over meat and vegetables. Add bouquet garni, cover with lid and braise in a slow oven for 1½-2 hours, ur until meat is tender. Remove string from Beef Olives and adjust consistency and flavour of sauce, if necessary, before serving.

BEEF CURRY

Serves: 6-8

2 large onions
·5 cm (2 inch) piece fresh ginger
3-4 cloves garlic
4 tablespoons ghee, butter or margarine
4 tablespoons curry powder
1 teaspoon turmeric
2 teaspoons black mustard seeds
    (optional)
2 teaspoons salt
1 tablespoon vinegar
1.5 kg (3 lb) blade or stewing steak
2 fresh chillies, chopped and seeded
3 ripe tomatoes

Finely chop onions, peel and grate ginger and crush garlic; heat ghee, butter or margarine in saucepan and fry these ingredients until golden. Add curry powder, turmeric and mustard seeds and fry gently over a low heat for 2-3 minutes. Add salt and vinegar and stir well. Cut steak into chunky cubes, add to curry mixture and fry, stirring to coat meat well. Add seeded chillies and chopped tomatoes. Cover pan and simmer on very low heat for about 2 hours. To thicken, cook over high heat, uncovered, until reduced. Serve with accompaniments.

Note: Beef Curry can also be cooked in a lidded casserole dish in a moderately slow oven for 1½-2 hours or until tender.

STUFFED BEEF FAN

Serves: 8-10

Seasoning
2 cups soft white breadcrumbs
¾ cup milk
2 onions, finely chopped
4 tablespoons butter, margarine or oil
125 g (4 oz) mushrooms, finely chopped
125 g (4 oz) lamb's liver, minced
salt and pepper
½ teaspoon each of mixed spices and
    thyme
1 egg yolk

Beef
1.5-2 kg (3-4 lb) rump or sirloin steak, in
    one piece
125 g (4 oz) bacon rashers
4 tablespoons butter, margarine or oil
1 onion, finely chopped
125 g (4 oz) mushrooms, sliced
½ cup white wine
hot beef consommé, or stock (see page
    154) or water and stock cubes
¼ cup Madeira

To make seasoning: Soak the breadcrumbs in the milk then squeeze to remove the excess liquid. Cook the onions in melted butter, margarine or oil until soft but not brown, then add breadcrumbs, mushrooms and liver. Cook over a low heat for a few minutes. Season with salt, pepper, mixed spices, thyme and put aside to cool. Add the egg yolk and mix well.

To prepare Beef Fan: Trim the meat and slice vertically so that it forms 10-12 slices, still joined at the base. Spread the stuffing between slices of meat, keeping any surplus aside. Wrap stuffed meat in bacon rashers, and tie loosely with string. Heat the butter, margarine or oil in a casserole dish, add the meat, and cook over a medium heat until bacon and meat brown. Add the onion, mushrooms and white wine. When wine is boiling, lower the flame and cover. Simmer 3-3½ hours or until tender, adding, if necessary, a little hot consommé, stock, or water and stock cubes. Ten minutes before serving, stir in remaining stuffing and Madeira. When cooked, lift the meat onto a hot dish and remove the string. Stir the liquid in the casserole dish and strain into a sauce boat to serve separately.

Note: Stuffed Beef Fan can also be cooked in a lidded casserole in a moderately slow oven for 3-3½ hours or until tender.

POT ROAST STUFFED STEAK

Serves: 6-8

Stuffing
1 small onion, chopped
2 tablespoons butter or margarine
1 cup soft breadcrumbs
½ teaspoon mixed herbs
½ teaspoon salt
pinch of pepper

Pot Roast
1.5-2 kg (3-4 lb) corner cut of topside
3 tablespoons dripping or oil
1 onion, chopped
1 carrot, chopped
1 cup water or beef stock (see page 154)

To make stuffing: Cook the onion in the butter or margarine in a saucepan until tender and lightly browned. Add the breadcrumbs, herbs and seasonings and mix together.

To prepare Pot Roast: Cut a pocket in the meat. Lightly press the stuffing into the pocket. Close the opening with meat skewers or by sewing it with a large needle and heavy cotton. Heat the dripping in a large heavy saucepan and brown the meat on all sides. Add vegetables and fry till browning on the edges. Pour off the fat. Add the water or stock, cover and cook gently for 2½-3 hours. Add a little more water if necessary during cooking. Serve hot with gravy from the saucepan.

Note: Pot Roast Stuffed Steak may also be cooked in a lidded casserole dish in a moderately slow oven for 1½-2 hours or until tender.

OXTAIL AU LIFFEY

Serves: 4-6

2 oxtails, cut into segments by the butcher
1 tablespoon oil
2 carrots, chopped
1 onion, chopped
1 clove garlic
few drops Worcestershire sauce
1 tablespoon paprika
3 bay leaves
12 peppercorns
6 whole cloves
1½ cups stout
salt to taste
water to cover
1½ tablespoons butter or margarine
1½ tablespoons plain flour

Brown the oxtail in a little oil and its own fat. Add carrots, onion, garlic, Worcestershire sauce, paprika, bay leaves, peppercorns, cloves, stout and salt to taste. Add enough water to cover.

Simmer gently for 3-4 hours or until very tender. This is quicker if you've got a pressure cooker — it only needs 1-2 hours cooking. When cooked, cool and chill in the fridge. (Oxtail is better if cooked the day before eating in which case you can leave it in the fridge overnight.)

Before serving remove the solidified fat from the mixture and bring back to the boil. Mix together the butter or margarine and flour and add a little at a time to the simmering stew to thicken it. Cook for a further 30 minutes to heat through and serve with mashed potatoes and green peas.

Note: Oxtail au Liffey can also be cooked in a lidded casserole dish in a moderately slow oven for 3-4 hours.

METRIC MEATBALLS

Serves: 3-4

500 g (1 lb) minced beef
1 onion, finely chopped
1 egg
½ cup soft white breadcrumbs
2 rashers bacon, finely chopped
2 tablespoons parsley, chopped
2 tablespoons tomato ketchup
salt and pepper
3 tablespoons plain flour
fat or oil for frying
1 cup tomato juice
salt and pepper
1 tablespoon lemon juice
1 teaspoon Worcestershire sauce

Mix together meat, onion, egg, breadcrumbs, bacon, parsley, tomato sauce, salt and pepper. When combined, wet hands and form mixture into balls about the size of golf balls. Roll these in about 3 tablespoons flour to coat, then fry in hot fat or oil until well browned. Place in a small saucepan and add tomato juice, salt and pepper, lemon juice and Worcestershire sauce. Cover with a lid and simmer gently for about 30 minutes or until cooked. These meatballs make a good meal served with fluffy mashed potatoes or buttery noodles and green beans tossed with butter and parsley.

Note: Metric Meatballs can also be cooked in a lidded casserole dish in a moderately slow oven for 30-45 minutes or until tender.

DOLMADES
(Stuffed Vine Leaves)

Serves: 3-4
Oven temperature: moderate

16 fresh or tinned vine leaves
500 g (1 lb) lean minced beef
½ cup long grain rice
2 onions, finely chopped
1 clove garlic, crushed
2 teaspoons salt
½ teaspoon pepper
1 teaspoon dried oregano leaves
1 tablespoon chopped fresh mint
2½ cups beef stock (see page 154) or
    water and beef stock cubes

If using fresh vine leaves, choose medium-sized leaves that are not too dark in colour. Large, dark leaves are tough. Snip off stems with kitchen scissors, wash well, place in a bowl and pour boiling water over to soften. If using tinned vine leaves in brine, wash in warm water before filling.

To prepare filling, combine all remaining ingredients except stock, mixing thoroughly. Divide mixture into 16 portions and shape into small sausages. Place one leaf at a time on a wooden board, shiny side downwards and place a portion of meat filling on leaf, near the stem. Fold over sides of leaf, then roll up to tip, enclosing meat completely. Pack rolls close together, seam side down, in neat rows in a heavy saucepan or casserole dish. If necessary, put a second layer on top of the first. Pour stock into pan and cover with lid. Bring slowly to simmering point and simmer gently for 45-60 minutes, or cook in a moderate oven for about 45-60 minutes.

LASAGNE NAPOLI

Serves: 6-8
Oven temperature: moderate

375 g (12 oz) lasagne
2 tablespoons olive oil or salad oil
1 onion, finely chopped
2 cloves garlic, crushed
500 g (1 lb) minced beef
1 x 125 g (4 oz) tin sliced mushrooms
1 x 425 g (15 oz) can tomatoes
¾ cup tomato paste
1½ teaspoons oregano or marjoram
salt
¾ cup water or red wine
1 egg
1 x 250 g (10 oz) packet frozen
spinach, chopped or puréed
1 cup cottage cheese
½ cup grated Parmesan cheese
salt
250 g (8 oz) Mozzarella or Cheddar
cheese

Lasagne is thick and hearty and the sauce is rich. The dish should not be soupy or dry when ready to serve.

Cook lasagne in boiling water until just tender. Do not drain. Add 1-2 cups cold water and leave till ready for layering. This prevents lasagne from sticking together.

Heat 1 tablespoon of oil in a frying pan and fry onion, garlic and meat until browned. Stir in mushrooms, tomatoes, tomato paste, oregano, salt to taste and water, or wine if preferred. Simmer for 20 minutes. Meanwhile, blend together egg, thawed spinach, cottage cheese, Parmesan cheese, remaining oil, and salt. Pour half the meat sauce into an oblong baking dish. Cover with a layer of lasagne. Spread spinach mixture over lasagne. Cover with another layer of lasagne then with remaining meat sauce. Top with a lid, or aluminium foil, and bake in a moderate oven for 40-50 minutes. Cut Mozzarella or Cheddar cheese into strips. Remove cover and place strips of cheese on top of lasagne. Bake until cheese melts and bubbles. Serve hot.

MINCED BEEF AND NOODLE CASSEROLE

Serves: 4-6
Oven temperature: moderate

170-250 g (6-8 oz) egg noodles
1 tablespoon oil or dripping
500 g (1 lb) minced beef
1 clove garlic, finely chopped
2 beef stock cubes
2 cups water
½ cup tomato ketchup
¼ teaspoon dried mixed herbs
2 tablespoons cornflour
salt, pepper and sugar
170 g (6 oz) matured Cheddar cheese,
grated
½ teaspoon paprika

Cook the noodles in boiling salted water until tender but not soft. Drain and rinse. Melt the oil or dripping in a large frypan and brown the minced beef and garlic, stirring frequently during cooking. Dissolve the beef cubes in the water and add to the browned meat. Add the tomato ketchup and herbs, cover, and simmer 15 minutes. Thicken with cornflour blended with a little cold water. Taste and season carefully.

Put half the cooked noodles in an ovenproof dish. Cover with half the meat then half the cheese. Repeat layers with the remaining ingredients finishing with a layer of cheese. Sprinkle top with paprika and cover tightly. Bake in a moderate oven for 1 hour. Serve with a green salad or cooked green vegetable.

CABBAGE ROLLS ABICAIR

Serves: 2-3

8 large green cabbage leaves
500 g (1 lb) minced steak (or raw minced
  lamb)
1 onion, chopped
½ cup raw rice
salt and pepper
1-2 tablespoons chopped mint
1 clove garlic, crushed
lemon juice

Pack cabbage leaves into a basin, cover with boiling water and leave to one side for 5 minutes to soften. Drain, reserving the water. Mix together all other ingredients, except lemon juice and 1 tablespoon of the mint. When cabbage leaves have cooled slightly place a few spoonfuls of meat mixture in each one. Fold over sides then roll up like a small parcel. Secure with toothpicks. Pack rolls into a saucepan with joins downwards, so parcels stay rolled. Top with reserved cabbage water. Add remaining mint and salt to taste. Cover with a lid and gently simmer 1-1½ hours. Remove to serving dish and sprinkle with lemon juice. Serve hot or cold.

Variation: Use 1 can of tomatoes instead of cabbage water for a more flavourful sauce.

Note: Cabbage Rolls Abicair can also be cooked in a lidded casserole dish in a moderately slow oven for 1½-2 hours or until tender.

Mary had a little lamb and this is how she cooked it

There's more to lamb than grilled chops and good old roast — so much more!

In the old days our tastes barely extended beyond family favourites like Irish Stew and Lancashire Hot Pot. But that's all history. Our tastes are now more cosmopolitan. Visitors and immigrants have extended our culinary range far beyond a simple Anglo-Saxon diet. They've introduced some luscious recipes for lamb, such as spicy curries and melting Greek moussaka. The spices used were once needed for more than flavourings; they were necessary to turn sinewy, tough mutton into something appetising.
Imagine the same methods applied to the tender, succulent lamb available these days.

CHOPPING AN ONION

1 Halve the onion before peeling. The cut edge makes it easier to peel. I always leave a few of the tough outside leaves attached to the onion, as they give you something to grip onto when the chopping is almost through. Trim off pointed end then slice across the onion horizontally, almost to the root.

2 Cut down in vertical slices, being careful not to cut through the root, but to leave the slices still attached to the onion.

3 Now slice down across the whole onion. This method of chopping gives the finest dice with the least amount of effort.

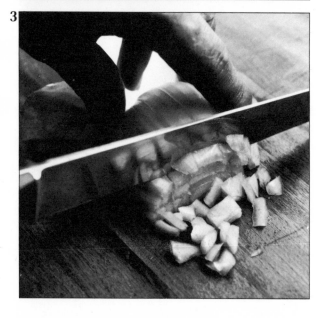

Left: Moussaka (page 44);
right: Sally's Stunning Chops (page 44)

LIVVY'S LAMB CASSEROLE

Serves: 6-8
Oven temperature: moderate

3 onions, finely chopped
2 tablespoons butter or margarine
2 tablespoons oil
1 stick celery, chopped
2 carrots, diced
250 g (½ lb) button mushrooms, sliced
2 cloves garlic, crushed
handful chopped parsley
1.5 kg (3 lb) best end lamb chops, lightly
   cooked
seasoned flour for tossing
salt and pepper
3 tomatoes, chopped
1 glass red wine
2 bay leaves
chicken or beef stock, (see page 154), or
   water and stock cubes
chopped parsley to garnish

Fry onions in mixture of butter or margarine and oil till softened, add celery, carrots, mushrooms, crushed garlic and parsley. Fry slowly for about 5 minutes. Toss chops in seasoned flour to coat and then add to pan. Cook for 10 minutes on each side. Add salt and pepper, tomatoes, wine and bay leaves, then top up with enough chicken or beef stock to cover, or use water with stock cubes. Cover and cook in a moderate oven for about 2 hours or until tender. Before serving sprinkle liberally with parsley.

Variation: Baby new potatoes may be added to the casserole during the last 30 minutes of cooking, in which case you may need to add a little more stock. Alternatively, serve with rice.

CIDER LAMB RAGOÛT

Serves: 6-8
Oven temperature: moderately slow

1 kg (2 lb) lamb shoulder chops
3 tablespoons oil
3 cups medium sweet cider
2 large onions, sliced
1 cup diced celery
1 large can whole tomatoes (about 840 g
   or 30 oz)
2 teaspoons salt
1 teaspoon cinnamon
¼ teaspoon black pepper
water
2 large carrots, cut in chunks
3 large potatoes, cut in large cubes
2-3 tablespoons cornflour

Fry the lamb chops in heated oil in a large heavy saucepan till brown. Remove meat and drain. Add 2 cups cider to the saucepan and boil, scraping to loosen the brown crusty bits and pieces. Return the chops to pan, add onions, celery, tomatoes, salt, cinnamon, pepper and water to cover. Top with a lid and simmer gently for 1 hour or until the lamb is almost tender. Add carrots and potatoes and cook until vegetables are tender. Blend cornflour with remaining cup cider. Stir into lamb and vegetable mixture and cook until thickened. Test seasoning, adjusting if necessary.

Note: Cider Lamb Ragoût can also be cooked in a lidded casserole dish in a moderately slow oven for 1-1½ hours or until tender.

Ragoût of Lamb (page 38)

RAGOÛT OF LAMB

Serves: 4

750 g (1½ lb) boned lamb
125 g (4 oz) thick bacon rashers
1 tablespoon olive oil
1 tablespoon oil, butter or margarine
500 g (1 lb) baby onions, peeled
2-3 carrots, cut in chunks
1 clove garlic, chopped
1½ teaspoons salt
freshly ground black pepper
½ teaspoon marjoram
½ teaspoon dried rosemary spikes or ¼
   teaspoon ground rosemary
2 tablespoons tomato paste
¼ cup dry red wine or stout
1 cup beef stock (see page 154) or water

Trim excess fat from lamb and cut into chunks. Chop bacon, place in pan in which ragoût is to be cooked and cover with water. Bring to the boil, drain off water, return to heat with 1 tablespoon olive oil added and fry bacon until crisp. Drain and put aside. Brown lamb in oil, butter or margarine and fat mixture in pan, lift out. Add onions, carrots and garlic to pan and fry until soft over a low heat, then add seasoning, herbs, tomato paste, wine and stock. Stir well and return bacon and lamb to pan. Cover and simmer for 1 hour or until lamb is tender. Sauce should be thick enough at the end of this time. Serve hot with new, creamed or fried potatoes and a green vegetable or a tossed salad.

Note: Ragoût of Lamb may also be cooked in a lidded casserole in a moderately slow oven for 1-1½ hours or until tender.

APRICOT LAMB STEW

Serves: 4

750 g (1½ lb) boned shoulder of
   lamb, or mutton
2 tablespoons oil, butter or margarine
1 onion, chopped
1 teaspoon salt
freshly ground black pepper
¾ cup water
1 cup dried apricots
3 teaspoons sugar
2 tablespoons pine nuts or walnuts, if
   available

Trim excess fat from lamb and cut into chunks. Heat oil, butter or margarine in a heavy pan or flameproof casserole and brown the meat on all sides, cooking it in two lots. Lift meat out and keep aside. Reduce heat and fry onion until soft. Return meat to pan and add salt, pepper and water. Cover and simmer for 30 minutes. Add apricots and sugar and simmer until tender (a further 45 minutes for lamb, 1 hour or more for mutton). Add pine nuts or walnuts, if available, 5 minutes before end of cooking time. Serve Apricot Lamb Stew hot with boiled rice and a green vegetable.

Note: Stir stew occasionally during later part of cooking as apricots tend to stick to pan. This is meant to be a thick stew. Pine nuts are available in health food stores.

Apricot Lamb Stew can also be cooked in a lidded casserole in a moderately slow oven for 1½-2 hours or until tender.

MIKE'S CURRY

Serves: 4-6
Oven temperature: moderately slow

1 kg (2 lb) lean lamb
2 tablespoons olive oil
¼-½ cup canned curry paste, or to taste
2 onions, chopped
2 courgettes, sliced
2 cloves garlic, crushed
3 tomatoes, chopped
2 apples, peeled, cored and diced
½ cup water

Trim the lamb, removing all fat and gristle, and cut into cubes. Heat oil in a large saucepan and fry lamb until browned. Add curry paste and onions and fry until softened. Add courgettes, garlic, tomatoes and apples. Add water if necessary, but the vegetables will generally supply enough. Top with a tight lid and either cook over a very slow heat or in a moderately slow oven until tender — about 1½-2 hours. When cooked, allow to cool and then leave in the fridge overnight to let the flavours blend. Reheat and serve with boiled or fried rice and side dishes, such as fried papadoms, sliced onion with yoghurt and mint, chutney, tomatoes, and pineapple.

IRISH STEW

Serves: 4
Oven temperature: moderately slow

750 g (1½ lb) best end neck chops
2 tablespoons plain flour
1½ teaspoons salt
¼ teaspoon pepper
2 onions, sliced
750 g (1½ lb) potatoes, thickly sliced
2 tablespoons chopped parsley

Trim chops and coat with flour seasoned with salt and pepper. Place a layer of sliced onions in bottom of an ovenproof casserole then cover with half the chops. Repeat layers, finishing with a layer of onions. Add cold water just to cover. Place lid on casserole and cook in a moderately slow oven for 1¼ hours. Remove from oven and place potatoes on top of stew, then cook for a further 45 minutes. Serve hot, sprinkled with chopped parsley. Traditionally served with boiled root vegetables such as parsnips, and a green vegetable.

LAMB AND VEGETABLE CASSEROLE

Serves: 4
Oven temperature: moderate

750 g (1½ lb) best end neck or chump
    chops
1 tablespoon plain flour
1½ teaspoons salt
freshly ground black pepper
1 tablespoon oil, butter or margarine
1 large onion, sliced
1 clove garlic, crushed
1 green and 1 red pepper, sliced
2 tablespoons tomato paste
4 tomatoes, chopped
1 cup beef stock (see page 154) or
    water and stock cube
250 g (8 oz) courgettes, sliced
1 cup fresh, shelled peas
chopped parsley for garnish

Trim chops, removing excess fat and any gristle. Coat with seasoned flour and brown over a high heat in a heavy frying pan or flameproof casserole in hot oil, butter or margarine. Lift meat out and place it directly into an ovenproof casserole or keep it aside if using a flameproof casserole. Add onion and garlic to pan and fry over a reduced heat until soft. Add sliced pepper, fry for 1-2 minutes, then add tomato paste, chopped tomatoes and stock. Return chops to flameproof casserole or pour liquid and vegetables over chops in the ovenproof casserole. Cover and cook in a moderate oven for 1½ hours. Add sliced courgettes and green peas and cook a further 30 minutes. Sprinkle with chopped parsley, and serve from the casserole at the table. Baked jacket potatoes go well with it.

LAMB CURRY

Serves: 4

750 g (1½ lb) boneless lamb or mutton
2 tablespoons oil, butter or margarine
1 onion, chopped
1 clove garlic
1-2 tablespoons curry powder
½ green pepper, finely chopped
½ cup sliced celery
½ teaspoon ground ginger
¼ teaspoon paprika
½ cup coconut milk (see page 157)
½ cup beef stock (see page 154), or
    water and stock cube
¼ cup seedless raisins
3 tablespoons yoghurt

Cut lamb into chunks, and trim off any fat. Heat oil, butter or margarine in a heavy saucepan and fry meat, onion and garlic over a low heat. Remove meat to one side. Stir the curry powder into the onion mixture and cook for 5 minutes, then return meat to pan and cook for a further 10 minutes. Add pepper, celery, ginger, paprika, coconut milk, stock, or water and stock cube and raisins. Stir well to blend, cover and simmer for 1½-2 hours or until meat is tender. Stir in yoghurt and heat through without boiling. For a real curry meal serve with boiled rice, mango chutney, papadoms and a variety of sambals.

Note: Lamb Curry can also be cooked in a lidded casserole dish in a moderately slow oven for 1½-2 hours or until tender.

SPICED CHOPS

Serves: 4-6
Oven temperature: moderately slow

6 lamb leg chops
2 tablespoons brown sugar
2 tablespoons plain flour
2 tablespoons vinegar
2 tablespoons tomato ketchup
¼ teaspoon ground ginger
½ teaspoon curry powder
½ teaspoon dry mustard
½ teaspoon mixed spice
1 teaspoon salt
pinch of pepper
1½ cups water
2 tablespoons sherry (optional)

Trim the fat from the chops and place them in a casserole. Mix the remaining ingredients together and pour over the chops. Leave to marinate for 2-3 hours. Cover the casserole and bake in a moderately slow oven for 2 hours.

TESS'S GREEK LAMB AND MACARONI CASSEROLE

Serves: 4
Oven temperature: moderately slow

750 g (1½ lb) boneless lamb, cut into
    small cubes
2 tablespoons oil
freshly ground black pepper
2 cloves garlic, crushed
1 large onion, chopped
1½ teaspoons salt
2 medium tomatoes, skinned and
    chopped
1 tablespoon tomato paste
2 cups hot stock (see page 154) or water
    and stock cubes
1 bay leaf
3 whole cloves
¼ teaspoon cinnamon
1 teaspoon sugar
2 cups macaroni
1 cup water
¾ cup diced Cheddar cheese

Combine lamb, oil and pepper in a wide shallow casserole dish. Bake in a hot oven for 15 minutes to brown meat, stirring occasionally. Lower heat to moderately slow and add garlic and onions and cook for a further 15 minutes. Combine salt, tomatoes, tomato paste, stock, bay leaf, cloves, cinnamon and sugar and pour over the meat. Cover and bake in a moderately slow oven for 45 minutes. Add macaroni and water and cook a further 35 minutes, or until macaroni is tender. Sprinkle surface with cheese cubes and return to the oven until the cheese melts. This casserole goes well with a Greek salad made from lettuce, cucumber, olives and tomato slices.

LAMB IN SOUR CREAM

Serves: 4-6
Oven temperature: moderate

1 kg (2 lb) neck of lamb
plain flour
pinch of tarragon, thyme and caraway
    seeds
2 tablespoons butter or margarine
salt and pepper
1 cup beef stock (see page 154), or water
    and stock cube
1 onion, chopped
juice of ½ lemon
1 cup sour cream
2 tablespoons dry white wine

Trim fat off lamb and cut into bite-sized pieces. Coat with flour, sprinkle with herbs, then brown meat in butter or margarine. Season, add all other ingredients and cook, covered, in a moderate oven for 1½ hours or until tender.

POT O' CHOPS

Serves: 2-4
Oven temperature: moderately slow

1 onion, sliced
1 rasher bacon, diced
2 tablespoons butter or margarine
4 lamb chump chops
2 tablespoons plain flour
1 teaspoon salt
1 teaspoon mustard
1 tablespoon brown sugar (white will do)
½ cup vinegar
1½ cups stockpot soup or beef and vegetable soup
¼ cup tomato paste (optional)

Brown onion and bacon in 1 tablespoon butter or margarine, in a flameproof casserole and put aside. Wipe chops with damp cloth, coat with flour and brown in remainder of butter or margarine. Return onion and bacon and all other ingredients to casserole, bring to boil, then cover with a lid and cook in a moderately slow oven for 1½ hours or until meat is tender.

LAMB CHOPS ROSEMARY

Serves: 4
Oven temperature: slow

4 lamb chump chops
2 tablespoons plain flour
2 cloves garlic, chopped
1 onion, chopped
1 green pepper, chopped
2 teaspoons rosemary, chopped
6 juniper berries, lightly crushed (optional)
1 teaspoon black peppercorns
2 teaspoons grated lemon peel
1 tablespoon tomato paste
1½ cups dry white wine

Roll chops in flour and place in a casserole with the other ingredients. Cover with lid and bake in a slow oven for 1½ hours. Add a little water during cooking if necessary. Serve hot with boiled rice.

BRAISED LAMBS' TONGUES

Serves: 4
Oven temperature: moderate

8 lambs' tongues
2 tablespoons dripping or lard
2 carrots, chopped
2 onions, chopped
1½ cups canned mushroom soup
¼ cup dry sherry (optional)
2 cups beef stock (see page 154) or water and beef stock cube
2 tablespoons tomato paste
bouquet garni (see page 82)

Wash and trim tongues. Place in cold water to cover and bring to the boil. Strain. Melt dripping or lard in a flameproof casserole. Add carrot and onion and fry till softened. Add prepared tongues with remaining ingredients. Bring to the boil and skim. Cover and cook in a moderate oven for 1½ hours. Remove tongues, skin and cut into long slices. Strain sauce. Serve tongues on a warm serving dish, coated with the sauce.

DELICIOUS LAMB CHOPS

Serves: 4-5

6-7 lamb chump chops, cut thickly
1 onion, finely chopped
½ cup blackcurrant jelly
finely grated rind and juice of 1 lemon
1 tablespoon fruit chutney
1 tablespoon tomato ketchup
½ cup water

If necessary, remove skin from chops. Cut fat in a few places. Heat a heavy pan, add chops and cook until well browned on both sides, turning frequently, then remove from pan. Fry onion in lamb fat until lightly browned. Add blackcurrant jelly, lemon rind and juice, sauces and water. Heat until blended then replace chops. Cover and simmer until cooked, about 30-40 minutes, turning a couple of times. If sauce is not thick enough, uncover for last 10 minutes of cooking time.

Note: Delicious Lamb Chops can also be cooked in a shallow lidded casserole dish in a moderately slow oven for 40-50 minutes or until tender.

LEG CHOPS WITH APRICOTS

Serves: 4
Oven temperature: moderately slow

4 mutton leg chops
2 tablespoons plain flour for coating
1 tablespoon dripping, butter or
  margarine
3 tablespoons dried apricots
¾ cup water
1 tablespoon brown sugar
½ teaspoon curry powder
½ teaspoon dry mustard
½ teaspoon ground ginger
½ tablespoon plain flour
1 tablespoon vinegar
¼ cup tomato ketchup

Trim as much fat as possible from the chops, coat with flour, and brown them on both sides in dripping, butter or margarine in a frying pan. Drain on kitchen paper, and arrange them one layer deep in an ovenproof dish. Add the dried apricots, chopped or whole, to the water in a small saucepan. Simmer, covered, for 10 minutes. Mix the remaining ingredients in a small mixing bowl. Pour enough hot water from the apricots onto them to make a thin smooth paste. Pour this mixture back into the saucepan with the apricots and bring to the boil, stirring constantly. Pour over the chops, cover tightly and cook in a moderately slow oven for about 2½ hours. Turn the chops occasionally during cooking so that all parts of them come in contact with the liquid. There should be 2-3 tablespoons liquid left for serving. Add extra liquid during cooking if the lid is not tightly fitting.

Before serving chops drain off the liquid and remove any fat. Pour the fat-free liquid back over the chops. Serve chops with mashed potatoes, cabbage and pumpkin, or with baked potatoes, mashed swede and green peas.

Note: This is a good method of cooking tough chops. If tender chops are used cooking time must be reduced. This dish may be left to cool then reheated, which allows for easy removal of fat.

SALLY'S STUNNING CHOPS

Serves: 6-8
Oven temperature: moderately slow

12-16 lamb chump chops
2-4 cloves garlic
sprigs of rosemary or dried rosemary
2 packets goulash sauce mix
1 cup tomato juice
⅓ cup brown sugar
salt and pepper, if necessary

Cut slits in the fleshy part of the chops with a sharp knife. Slice garlic cloves into thin slivers and push a sliver of garlic and a spike of rosemary into each slit. Arrange chops in a casserole dish. Make up goulash sauce mix according to the directions on the packet using 1 cup tomato juice instead of water. Pour over the meat. Sprinkle with brown sugar and cover. Bake in a moderately slow oven for 1½-2 hours or till well cooked. Turn a few times during cooking.

Note: This dish can also be made unseasoned, without the rosemary or garlic.

MOUSSAKA

Serves: 4-6
Oven temperature: moderate

Meat Sauce
3 rashers bacon, diced
2 tablespoons butter or margarine
2 tablespoons oil
1 onion, chopped
1 carrot, sliced
1 stick celery, chopped
500 g (1 lb) minced lamb or steak
250 g (8 oz) chicken livers, chopped
2 tablespoons tomato paste
1 bay leaf
2 cloves garlic, crushed
½ cup red wine
1-2 stock cubes
strip lemon peel
1 cup water
½ teaspoon oregano or mixed herbs
½ cup cream

Moussaka
1 small aubergine, sliced
¼ cup oil
6 tomatoes, sliced

Cheese Sauce
2 tablespoons butter or margarine
2 tablespoons plain flour
1 cup milk
salt and pepper to taste
½ cup grated Cheddar cheese
2 eggs, separated

To make the meat sauce. Fry bacon in butter, or margarine and oil until fat starts to run. Add onion, carrot and celery and cook till soft. Add mince and livers and cook till brown. Add all remaining sauce ingredients except cream then cover and simmer for 40 minutes or until meat is tender. Remove lid and boil quickly until thickened. Mix a little hot sauce with cream then add to the rest of the sauce.

To make the moussaka. Slice the aubergine thickly and fry in oil until tender. Arrange a layer of aubergine in the base of a casserole dish. Top with a layer of tomato slices. Spread meat sauce over the top.

To make the cheese sauce. Melt butter in a saucepan, blend in flour until smooth. Add milk and bring to the boil, stirring continuously. Season to taste with salt and pepper. Remove from heat, add cheese and stir till melted. Add egg yolks and stir well. Whisk egg whites until stiff and gently fold into sauce.

Pour cheese sauce over the meat in the casserole. Bake in a moderate oven for 30-40 minutes or until hot and golden brown on top. Serve with a green salad.

Fair means or fowl

Chicken used to be a luxury, reserved only for feasts and festivities. Now it's one of the cheapest foods available, thanks to the twentieth century, assembly-line chicken farms. But just because the price is right, don't take that bird for granted. If it's cooked with the care and respect delicious meat deserves you'll be rewarded with rave reviews. The subtle delicate flavour of the flesh allows you to combine it with many other foods. You can add anything from a squirt of lemon, a slosh of red wine, dollops of cream, a scrape of mustard or a froth of beer and you'll get an exciting taste every time — each and every one superb.

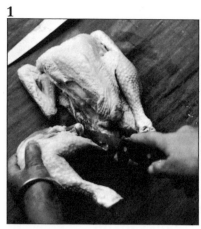

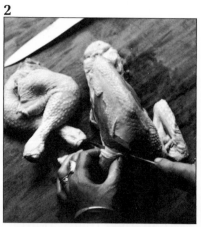

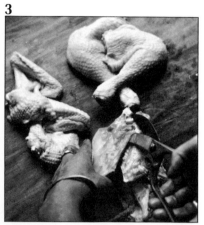

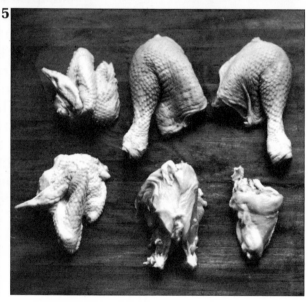

CUTTING A CHICKEN INTO PORTIONS

1 *Removing drumsticks.* Slice through the gristle around the joint, wiggling the leg to discover where the soft part of the joint is positioned. If desired flick out the oyster with the drumstick (this is the sweet morsel of meat tucked on the backbone). If the chicken is large cut each drumstick in half.

2 *Removing the wings.* Pinch up a decent amount of the breast near the wishbone, then slice down along the wishbone including the pinch of breast with the wing. This means the wing portion becomes a good meaty serving too.

3 With kitchen scissors or shears cut through the rib cage to remove the back from the breast. The back contains very little meat so it is best kept to make stock.

4 Cut through the breast in one or two places depending on the size of the bird.

5 *The End Result.* 6 pieces — 2 drumsticks, 2 wing portions and 2 breast portions. If the bird is large you get 9 portions — the breast is cut into 3 and the drumsticks halved.

CHICKEN À LA CARRIER

Serves: 2
Oven temperature: very slow

4 pieces of chicken
3 tablespoons French mustard
1 cup double cream

Place chicken pieces in a small casserole dish. Mix together the mustard and cream and pour over the chicken. Cover with a lid or foil and cook in a very slow oven for about 2 hours or till tender.

This seems a lot of mustard, but I assure you it's not too much. This casserole can be left in a very slow oven for much longer if convenient. Occasionally the sauce curdles, but will amalgamate again if stirred.

Serve with green beans and scalloped potatoes — it tastes scrumptious. This is one of my favourite recipes and I'm sure it will become one of yours, it's so simple.

CHICKEN CURRY

Serves: 4-6

2 onions
2 cloves garlic
2.5 cm (1 inch) piece fresh ginger
3 tablespoons ghee, butter or margarine
2 tablespoons curry powder
2 large ripe tomatoes
2 teaspoons paprika
2 cloves
7.5 cm (3 inch) stick cinnamon
2 cups coconut milk (see page 157)
2 teaspoons salt
2 fresh chillies
1 x 1.5 kg (3 lb) chicken
2 tablespoons cream or sour cream
1 tablespoon chopped fresh mint

Finely chop onions, crush garlic and grate ginger and cook gently together in hot ghee, butter or margarine in a saucepan until beginning to turn golden. Add curry powder and cook 3-4 minutes. Add skinned and diced tomatoes, paprika, cloves, cinnamon, coconut milk, salt and seeded chillies. Simmer, covered, about 15 minutes, then add chicken cut into serving pieces (see page 46) and simmer 30-40 minutes until chicken is tender. Remove chillies. Add cream and mint. Heat through and serve with accompaniments.

Note: Chicken Curry may also be cooked in a lidded casserole dish in a moderately slow oven for 1 hour or until tender.

CRUSTY CHICKEN

Serves: 3-4
Oven temperature: moderate

4-5 spring onions, chopped
4 tablespoons butter or margarine
¼ cup of bourbon or Scotch whiskey
½ cup seeded ripe olives, halved
½ teaspoon dried thyme
2 cups diced cooked chicken
1½ cups canned mushroom soup
½ cup evaporated milk
salt and pepper
1-2 teaspoons lemon juice
potato crisps

Fry the shallots in heated butter or margarine until just softened. Add the bourbon, olives, thyme and chicken and mix well. Stir in the mushroom soup and evaporated milk, then season with salt, pepper and lemon juice. Spoon into a greased casserole dish, cover and cook in a moderate oven for 10 minutes or until tender. Sprinkle with crushed potato crisps and cook another 10-15 minutes.

CHICKEN BAKED IN CREAM

Serves: 8-12
Oven temperature: moderate

**2 x 1.5 kg (3 lb) chickens, or 3 kg (6 lb)
  chicken pieces**
4 tablespoons butter or margarine
250 g (8 oz) mushrooms, sliced
2 cups double cream
⅔ cup dry white wine
salt and pepper
2 tablespoons chopped chives

Cut each chicken into quarters. Heat butter or margarine in frying pan and brown chicken pieces, then place in an ovenproof casserole. Add mushrooms to the pan and fry till softened. Mix cream and wine and add mushrooms, mix well. Pour over chicken. Cover with a lid and bake in a moderate oven for 1-1¼ hours or until chicken is tender. Season to taste with salt and pepper and cook for a further 5 minutes. Sprinkle with chopped chives and serve with boiled rice.

DUCKLING WITH ORANGE AND RED PEPPER

Serves: 4
Oven temperature: moderately hot

1 x 1.5 kg (3 lb) duck
2 tablespoons butter or margarine
1 sprig fresh thyme
1 bay leaf
2 parsley stalks
2 onions, thinly sliced
salt
¼ teaspoon freshly ground white pepper
¼ cup dry red wine
**1 cup chicken stock (see page 154) or
  water and chicken stock cube**
1 large orange
1 large red pepper
2 teaspoons arrowroot
paprika
1 teaspoon chopped parsley

Prepare duck for cooking. Mix together 1 tablespoon butter or margarine plus the herbs. Place inside the duck and truss. Rub the skin over with a little butter or margarine and fry the onions in the rest of the fat. Place duck and onions in a casserole with salt and white pepper. Pour wine over the duck along with the stock. Braise gently in a moderately hot oven without a lid for about 1 hour, basting every 15 minutes. While duck is cooking, blanch the whole orange in boiling water for 5 minutes, cut in half and slice finely. Blanch and shred the pepper in the same way. Add orange slices and pepper to duck for final 30 minutes of cooking. Take out duck, carve and keep hot. Strain and reduce the gravy to taste then thicken slightly with the arrowroot blended with a little cold water. Add paprika to taste and pour the gravy over the duck. Sprinkle with chopped parsley, and serve with baked jacket potatoes and a tossed green salad. Drink a red wine with the meal.

CHICKEN MARENGO

Serves: 4
Oven temperature: moderate

1 x 1.5 kg (3 lb) chicken
salt and pepper
2 tablespoons oil
2 tablespoons butter or margarine
12 mushroom caps
1 cup water
1 clove garlic, crushed
1 teaspoon plain flour
**2 large ripe tomatoes, skinned, seeded
  and chopped**
½ cup dry white wine
1 tablespoon tomato paste
salt and pepper

Cut chicken into portions (see page 46). Sprinkle with salt and pepper. Fry chicken pieces in a large frying pan in oil and butter or margarine until they are golden brown on all sides and almost cooked through. Remove the chicken and place in a casserole dish. In a small saucepan simmer the mushroom caps in 1 cup of salted water for 5 minutes, drain and put aside and reserve liquid. Add garlic and flour to the juices left in the frying pan and stir over a low heat for 1 minute. Add tomatoes and simmer for a few minutes, then add the wine and the mushroom liquor. Add tomato paste and salt and pepper to taste. Pour over chicken pieces. Top with a lid and bake in a moderate oven for 30-40 minutes or until tender. Add the mushrooms and return to oven and cook for a further 5 minutes. Serve with boiled rice or noodles.

JUNE BRONHILL'S EASY CHICKEN

Serves: 6-8
Oven temperature: moderate

2 medium cooked chickens
4 onions
2 green peppers
250 g (8 oz) mushrooms
2 tablespoons oil, butter or margarine
4 cloves garlic, crushed
1 can whole tomatoes (about 450 g or 15 oz)
salt and pepper to taste
mixed herbs, oregano or chicken seasoning mix (optional)

Tear chicken apart into nice big chunks. Leave legs and wings whole. Place in greased casserole. Make the sauce: slice onions into big rounds, remove cores from peppers and slice. Cut mushrooms into quarters. Fry onions and pepper in oil, butter or margarine until softened. Add mushrooms and garlic and fry till soft. Add tomatoes with their juice and smash around a bit to break up. Add salt and pepper to taste.

For extra flavour mixed herbs, oregano or chicken seasoning mix may be added. Bring sauce to the boil and simmer for 10-15 minutes. If the sauce is thin it may be thickened by boiling.

Pour the sauce over the chicken chunks and cover the casserole. Place in a moderate oven for about 30 minutes. Serve with potatoes, rice or spaghetti. This is even better the day after it has been made, if it is allowed to cool and then is stored in the fridge overnight.

CHICKEN IN A PAN

Serves: 4

1 x 1.5 kg (3 lb) chicken, cut into sections (see page 46)
juice of 2 large lemons
2 cups chicken stock (see page 154), or water and stock cubes
salt and pepper
3 onions, thickly sliced
2 carrots, sliced

Place chicken pieces in a frying pan, add lemon juice, chicken stock, or water and stock cubes, salt and pepper Allow to simmer for 45 minutes. Add onions and carrots and cook a further 15 minutes or until vegetables are cooked, but still crunchy.

Variations: There are many adaptations for this recipe. Substitute a cup of wine for one cup of stock. Vary the vegetables by adding small potatoes, celery, capsicum or turnips. The vegetable sauce can be used as an accompaniment to the chicken, or reserved and served as a soup later.

Note: Chicken in a Pan can also be cooked in a lidded casserole pot in a moderately slow oven for 1-1½ hours or until tender.

COCONUT CHICKEN

Serves: 6
Oven temperature: moderately slow

1½-2 cups coconut milk (see page 157)
6 chicken breasts
pinch mace or nutmeg
3-4 chicken stock cubes
salt and pepper
1 onion, finely sliced
2 tablespoons butter or margarine

Make up coconut milk as directed on page 157, but use only 3 cups water to 3 cups desiccated coconut. Alternatively, dissolve 60 g (2 oz) creamed coconut in 1½ cups hot water. Place chicken breasts in a shallow dish in one layer. Mix together coconut milk, mace or nutmeg and crumbled stock cubes and pour over the chicken breasts. Leave overnight in the fridge to allow the flavours to soak into the flesh, turning the breasts a few times if possible. Next day very gently fry onion slices in butter or margarine until very soft. Scrape over the chicken and stir well in. Cook gently in a moderately slow oven for 1-1¼ hours or till tender. Serve with simple boiled rice and crispy beans.

COQ AU VIN

Serves: 4

1 x 2 kg (4 lb) chicken
3 tablespoons butter or margarine
4 small onions
6 baby carrots, scrubbed and halved
4 rashers lean bacon, diced
2 tablespoons brandy
½ bottle dry red wine
1 cup chicken stock (see page 154) or
    water and chicken stock cube
salt and pepper
2 cloves garlic, crushed
bouquet garni (see page 82)
250 g (8 oz) button mushrooms
beurre manie (see page 157)

Cut chicken into serving pieces (see page 46). Melt butter or margarine in a flameproof casserole and fry onions, carrots and bacon until golden brown. Remove vegetables and bacon and in the remaining fat fry the pieces of chicken to a light golden colour on all sides. Pour warm brandy over the chicken, ignite and flame. Add red wine, chicken stock, salt and pepper to taste, garlic and bouquet garni. Bring to the boil, return the onions and bacon to the dish and add the whole mushrooms.

Cover the casserole, reduce heat and simmer gently for 40 minutes, or until the chicken is tender. Thicken with beurre manié. Remove bouquet garni and adjust flavourings if necessary. Serve with either fluffy white rice or small new potatoes.

Note: Coq au Vin may also be cooked in a lidded casserole dish in a slow oven for 40 minutes or until tender.

TURKEY FILLETS IN SOUR CREAM

Serves: 8
Oven temperature: moderate

fillets from a 6 kg (12 lb) turkey
seasoned fine breadcrumbs
2 eggs
2 tablespoons water
pinch of salt
butter or margarine for frying
1 tablespoon finely chopped onion
1 tablespoon finely chopped parsley
¼ cup water
1 cup sour cream
1 tablespoon plain flour

Remove the breast meat from turkey and cut each fillet into 8 uniform pieces. Dip pieces in seasoned fine breadcrumbs, then in eggs beaten with 2 tablespoons water and salt and finally dip again in crumbs. Brown the fillets on both sides in hot butter or margarine and transfer them to a baking dish. Sprinkle the turkey pieces with onion and parsley and add ¼ cup water. Pour sour cream over the fillets, cover the dish, and bake in a moderate oven for 15 minutes. Reduce heat to very slow and bake the fillets for 45 minutes or until they are tender. Remove cover and increase heat for the last few minutes of cooking to crispen. Transfer the turkey to a heated platter. Mix flour to a cream with cold water and stir into the sauce in the dish and cook for a few minutes. Strain over the turkey and serve hot.

CHICKEN PAPRIKA

Serves: 4-6

1 x 1 kg (2 lb) boiling chicken
⅓ cup seasoned flour
⅓ cup butter or margarine
125 g (4 oz) mushrooms, sliced
½ cup onions, chopped
2 teaspoons paprika
1 large bay leaf
1 x 285 g (10 oz) can condensed tomato
    soup
1 cup sour cream

Dust chicken with flour and brown in butter or margarine in a large pan. Drain off the fat. Stir in remaining ingredients except sour cream. Cover and simmer for 45 minutes or till tender. Remove bayleaf, blend in sour cream.

Note: Chicken Paprika can also be cooked in a lidded casserole dish in a moderately slow oven for ½-1 hour or until tender.

KATHERINE'S CHICKEN

Serves: 6-8
Oven temperature: moderately slow

2 tablespoons butter or margarine
2 tablespoons oil
1 x 2 kg (4 lb) chicken, cut into joints,
**   or 2 kg (4 lb) chicken pieces**
750 g (1½ lb) onions, chopped
125 g (4 oz) mushrooms, sliced (optional)
3 tablespoons extra butter or margarine
2 tablespoons plain flour
1 cup chicken stock (see page 154) or
**   water and stock cubes**
1 x 300 g (8 oz) carton sour cream
¼ cup tomato paste
2 tablespoons tomato ketchup, or to taste
2 teaspoons brown sugar
juice of ½ lemon
½-1 teaspoon freshly chopped or dried
**   thyme or tarragon**
salt and pepper to taste
stuffed olives for garnish

Heat butter or margarine and oil in a frying pan. When foam subsides add chicken pieces and fry until well browned. Remove and place in a casserole dish. Add chopped onions to pan and fry gently till softened, adding a little more fat if necessary. Add mushrooms and fry gently for a few minutes more. Scrape vegetables into casserole dish. Melt extra butter or margarine in frying pan. Sprinkle in flour and fry till straw coloured. Off the heat add stock, or water and stock cubes, and stir until combined. Simmer for a few minutes, scraping up the crusty bits and pieces in the pan. Remove from heat and add all other ingredients, mixing well. Pour over chicken pieces and stir to coat each piece well. Top with a lid and bake in a moderately slow oven for 1½ hours or until tender. Stir well before serving.

This casserole will last well if the meal has to be kept waiting. Turn oven down to low and the chicken can be left for a few hours longer. It will still be divine. Just before serving, garnish with stuffed olives.

MANGO CHICKEN

Serves: 4
Oven temperature: moderately slow

1 x 1.5 kg (3 lb) chicken
6 tablespoons butter or margarine
2 large onions, thinly sliced
6 slices fresh or tinned mango
grated nutmeg
3 strips of lemon rind
1 cup chicken stock (see below) or water
**   and stock cubes**
salt and pepper
juice of 1 lemon
½ cup double cream
paprika

Joint the chicken (see page 46) a few hours before cooking so that back and trimmings can be made into stock (see below). Fry chicken in half the butter or margarine until golden brown. Melt remaining fat in a saucepan or flameproof casserole and fry onion until golden. Add mango, increase heat and cook for 3-5 minutes. Add fried chicken, a little grated nutmeg, lemon rind, chicken stock, or water and stock cubes, salt and pepper to taste. Cover and cook in a moderately slow oven for 1 hour or until chicken is tender. Remove chicken and keep warm. Remove lemon rind from sauce and add lemon juice, season to taste. Stir in cream and allow to come to a gentle simmer. Pour sauce over chicken, sprinkle with paprika and serve with rice pilaf.

Variation: 2-3 peeled, sliced peaches may be used instead of the mango.

To make stock quickly: Put the chicken bones and trimmings in a pressure cooker, adding water to cover, a slurp of white wine, some chopped onion, parsley, carrot and a bay leaf and cook for 30 minutes. If not using a pressure cooker simmer for 1 hour.

DUCK IN RED WINE

Serves: 4
Oven temperature: moderately hot

Stock
3 tablespoons butter or margarine
neck, giblets, liver and wing tips and other trimmings from the duck
250 g (8 oz) beef fillet or chuck steak (chopped)
2 large onions, chopped
2 carrots, chopped
4 shallots, chopped
1 tablespoon plain flour
bay leaf, thyme and parsley tied together
1 bottle red wine
2 cups brown stock (see page 154) or beef consommé
salt and freshly ground pepper
2 cloves garlic, crushed
bouquet garni (see page 82)

Duck
1 x 2 kg (4 lb) duck
salt and pepper
½ cup sherry
2 tablespoons double cream
2 tablespoons grated Gruyère cheese

To make the stock: Melt butter or margarine in a heavy saucepan, add duck neck, giblets, wing tips and the chopped beef. Fry till brown, then add onions, carrots and shallots. Sprinkle with flour and cook till vegetables are softened and flour browns slightly. Add all other ingredients and bring to the boil. Lower heat, partly cover and simmer gently for 2-3 hours.

To prepare the duck: After trussing, rub the duck well with salt and pepper and partly cook in a moderately hot oven for 1 hour. Drain fat from the baking dish. Remove duck and cut into pieces: remove legs then cut breast into 2 or 3 pieces. Place duck pieces into an ovenproof dish, or into individual ramekins in which case allow one piece of breast and one leg per person. Chop up remaining carcass and return to the baking dish. Add sherry and simmer gently for a few minutes, scraping up the crusty bits and pieces stuck to the pan. Add all of this to the stock and simmer for a further 15 minutes. Strain the enriched stock, rubbing the vegetables through a sieve. (I'd use the blender, removing all the bones and the bouquet garni before blending, of course.) Stir the cream into the sauce. Pour the sauce over the duck pieces and sprinkle with cheese. Leave until ready to serve.

When ready to serve cook in a moderately slow oven for 20-30 minutes or until the cheese browns and the duck is well heated through and tender.

CHICKEN WITH CIDER

Serves: 4-6
Oven temperature: moderate

1 teaspoon salt
¼ teaspoon pepper
⅛ teaspoon garlic powder
½ cup plain flour
1 x 2 kg (4 lb) chicken, divided into sections
2 tablespoons melted butter or margarine
2 tablespoons oil
3 cooking apples, peeled, cored and quartered
1 leek, chopped
2 tablespoons sugar
2 tablespoons finely chopped preserved ginger
1½ cups medium sweet cider
½ cup water

Combine the salt, pepper, garlic powder and flour and coat the chicken pieces with this mixture. Heat the butter or margarine and oil in a frying pan, brown chicken pieces, a few at a time and transfer to a shallow flameproof casserole. Add apple quarters and leeks to frying pan, sprinkle with sugar and brown lightly. Arrange apple pieces around chicken in casserole, sprinkle with ginger. Add cider and water to the casserole. Cover and bake in a moderate oven for 45-50 minutes or until chicken is tender. Serve with potatoes and any other vegetables you wish.

Coq au Vin (page 50)

MEXICAN CHICKEN

Serves: 4
Oven temperature: moderate

1 x 2 kg (4 lb) chicken
1 tablespoon lemon juice
salt
2 tablespoons oil
1 large onion, finely diced
1 large clove of garlic, crushed
1 x 500 g (1 lb) tin tomatoes, drained and
    roughly chopped
1 tablespoon seedless raisins
4 prunes, stoned and cut in halves
60 g (2 oz) ham, diced
30 g (1 oz) butter or margarine, cut into
    small pieces
black pepper
¼ teaspoon cinnamon
¾ cup chicken stock (see page 154) or
    water and stock cubes
2 tablespoons almonds, cut into slivers
1 tablespoon pimento-stuffed olives, cut
    in slices

Cut the chicken into portions (see page 46), sprinkle with a little lemon juice and then salt. Heat the oil and fry the chicken until it is golden brown. Add the onion, garlic, tomatoes, raisins, prunes, ham, pieces of butter or margarine, pepper and cinnamon. Cook for about 10 minutes, shaking the pan occasionally. Then add the chicken stock, or water and stock cubes. Cook either on top of the stove or in the oven at a moderate heat — without a lid — until the chicken is tender. If it dries up during the cooking add a bit more chicken stock. Baste with the pan liquid every now and then. When cooked, serve on a heated platter and sprinkle with almonds and olive slices. Mexican Chicken tastes good with a rice side dish.

CHICKEN WITH LEMON

Serves: 6

1 x 2 kg (4 lb) chicken
1 lemon
salt and pepper
2 carrots, sliced
250 g (8 oz) onions, sliced
3 stalks celery, sliced
250 g (8 oz) mushrooms
4 tablespoons butter or margarine
½ cup dry sherry
¾ cup blanched almonds
1 egg
4 tablespoons double cream
salt and pepper

Rub chicken all over with cut side of half the lemon and season well with plenty of salt and pepper. Put the other half of the lemon inside chicken and tie the legs together. In a large pan bring enough water to the boil to cover the chicken. Add chicken, carrots, onions and celery. Simmer until chicken is tender, about 1¼-1½ hours. (If the bird is an old boiling fowl it will take 3 hours, in which case do not add vegetables until last hour of cooking.) Put chicken on a serving dish and keep warm. Reserve 1 cup chicken stock.

Slice the mushrooms and gently cook in butter or margarine until softened. Add reserved cup chicken stock, sherry and almonds and heat gently. Beat egg and cream, gradually blend in some of the hot stock, then pour into saucepan, stirring over a gentle heat until sauce thickens. Do not allow mixture to boil. Taste and add more salt and pepper if necessary. Pour sauce over chicken and serve.

Note: Chicken with Lemon can also be cooked in a lidded casserole dish in a moderately slow oven for 1-1½ hours or until tender (longer (3 hours) for a boiling fowl).

Cherry Veal (page 59)

CHICKEN INDIENNE

Serves: 6-8

2 x 1.5 kg (3 lb) roasting chickens
seasoned flour
125 g (4 oz) butter or margarine
3 medium onions
2 small apples, peeled and chopped
1 tablespoon curry powder
2 tablespoons plain flour
2 tablespoons chutney
1 teaspoon salt
pinch allspice
2 medium tomatoes
30 g (1 oz) dessicated coconut, soaked in
    a little warm water
2½ cups chicken stock (see page 154)
    (made from chicken carcasses), or use
    stock cubes and water
1 teaspoon lemon juice

Joint the chickens (see page 46) and use the carcasses to make the stock. Roll each piece of chicken in the seasoned flour. Melt half the butter or margarine in a pan and fry the chicken until golden brown. Drain well on kitchen paper. Melt the remaining butter or margarine in the same pan and fry the chopped onions until golden. Add the apple and fry lightly. Stir in the curry powder and flour and cook for 2 minutes. Add the chutney, salt, allspice, skinned and chopped tomatoes, the coconut and the stock, or water and stock cubes. Stir until boiling then add the fried chicken pieces. Cover with a lid and simmer gently for 45-60 minutes until the meat is tender. Flavour with lemon juice. Serve with freshly boiled rice and curry accompaniments such as chutney, pineapple, coconut, cashews or peanuts and crispy fried bacon.

Note: Chicken Indienne may also be cooked in a lidded casserole dish in a moderately slow oven for 45-60 minutes or until tender.

TURKEY WITH HAM AND OLIVES

Serves: 6-8
Oven temperature: slow

1 x 4 kg (8 lb) turkey
salt and pepper
250 g (8 oz) raw ham, chopped
24 olives
3 cloves garlic, sliced
6 peppercorns, crushed
1 tablespoon ground walnuts
½ teaspoon ground cloves
½ teaspoon ground cinnamon
muslin bag or aluminium foil
2 onions, quartered
2 oranges, sliced
3 sprigs parsley
1 bay leaf
¾ cup dry sherry

Wash and dry turkey and rub the body cavity with salt and pepper. Combine ham with olives, garlic and peppercorns and place inside bird. Skewer and truss the bird and rub the skin with a mixture of ground walnuts, ground cloves and cinnamon. Enclose the turkey in a muslin bag and tie the bag securely (or wrap securely in greased aluminium foil). Cook the turkey in simmering water to cover for approximately 1½ hours, depending on the age of the bird, or until it is almost tender. Remove the bag or foil and place turkey in a baking dish. Add onions, orange slices, parsley sprigs, bay leaf and dry sherry. Cover the dish and cook the bird in a slow oven until it is tender. Remove turkey, cut into serving pieces and arrange on a heated serving platter. Strain sauce from baking dish and pour it over the bird before serving.

CHICKEN DRUMSTICK

Serves: 2-3
Oven temperature: moderate

500 g (1 lb) chicken drumsticks
2 tablespoons plain flour
240 g (8 oz) fresh mushrooms, peeled and
    sliced
1 x 865 g (28 oz) can chicken and
    vegetable soup
parsley, chopped
1 bunch small cooked carrots to serve

Dip chicken pieces in flour and place in casserole. Slice the mushrooms and spread over the chicken, then pour the chicken and vegetable soup over both. Cover with lid and bake in a moderate oven for 1¼ hours or until chicken is tender. Sprinkle with parsley and serve with carrot rings.

Pork and veal for real

You might not be able to turn a sow's ear into a silk purse but you sure can turn it into a worthwhile casserole. After all, gristle is pure gelatine — that's why gristly pigs' heads or trotters are usually an essential ingredient of aspic and brawn. The same principle applies when using pork in casseroles. The richness of pork will turn the casserole sauce into a rich, glistening gravy.

But why stop at the sow's head? Cast your eye over the shoulders, leg, back and rump and you'll discover that fabulous dishes are just a chop, sprinkle and shake away.

Veal is a relatively new addition to many dinner tables — true veal, that is, which comes from baby calves between 5 and 12 weeks old, which are still milk-fed, so the flesh is almost white and the flavour is delicate.

In the past we ate veal that resembled baby beef, but since the war tastes have changed. We've got our friends from the Mediterranean to thank for this. In particular, our food is increasingly influenced by Italian cuisine. It doesn't stop at veal. There's garlic, aubergine, courgettes, peppers, olives, prosciutto and Parmesan cheese — and mixed together they make delicious Neapolitan Veal.

Mamma Mia, the Italian Mum, obviously knows a good meal when she sees it. She doesn't even need all these ingredients to make a knock-out dish. With just a clove of garlic and some tomatoes she can concoct a fabulous dish with veal.

These are just two of the many things you can do with versatile veal. Look at the following recipes and you'll see what I mean.

57

THICKENING A CASSEROLE

1 *Tossing meat in seasoned flour.* This is the most common method of thickening a casserole. The meat chunks are tossed in a flour mixture before they are fried until well browned. The flour may be seasoned or flavoured with any of the following: salt, pepper, lemon pepper, garlic salt, onion salt, dry mustard, sesame seeds, poppy seeds, packet seasonings, crumbled stock cubes or dry packet soups.

2 *Adding flour to vegetables.* If the meat chunks are fried without a flour coating, then the flour thickening is usually sprinkled over the vegetables while they are frying. Usually the flour is fried until golden brown to give a rich colour and flavour to the casserole gravy. A pinch of sugar speeds up this browning process.

3 *Cornflour thickening.* After the casserole has been cooked the liquid may be thickened with a cornflour paste. Just mix 1-2 tablespoons cornflour with enough cold water to make a mixture the thickness of thin cream. Add a little hot liquid from the casserole to the cornflour paste, then pour this mixture into the casserole gradually. Simmer after each addition and continue adding until casserole has thickened to the right consistency.

Arrowroot can also be used in this way, instead of cornflour. This is particularly useful if the mixture contains cream and should not be boiled, because arrowroot thickens below boiling point.

4
5 *Beurre manié.* This is another useful mixture for thickening a casserole after cooking. It is just flour and butter or margarine mixed together in equal quantities. Add small blobs of the beurre manié to the liquid while it simmers and stir it in. The butter allows the flour to melt into the liquid without causing lumps. Only add enough to thicken to the right consistency.

I make up a whole batch of beurre manie and store it in the fridge. It lasts indefinitely and may be used whenever a casserole is too thin.

PORK 'N PEACHES

Serves: 6
Oven temperature: moderate

6 pork chops
1 can peaches, drained, about 830 g (30 oz)
¼ cup peach syrup from can
2 onions, sliced
1 clove garlic, crushed
salt and pepper
3 tablespoons butter
1 cup double cream

Place all ingredients, except cream, in a shallow casserole dish, dotting top with butter. Top with a lid and bake in a moderate oven for 1½ hours or till tender, removing lid for the last ½ hour of cooking. Remove chops to a serving dish while you make the sauce.

Spoon off obvious excess fat. Tip the casserole contents into the blender and add cream. Blend till smooth and well combined. If you haven't a blender rub contents through a sieve and then add cream and stir well. Pour over chops and serve.

If desired this recipe can be completely prepared in advance and reheated in a moderately slow oven for about 10 minutes.

Variation: Use fresh peach slices instead of tinned ones. No liquid is necessary as enough comes out of the chops and peaches.

STUFFED PORK FILLET

Serves: 4

12 dried apricots
1 x 750 g (1½ lb) large, or 2 medium, pork fillets
1 cooking apple
2 tablespoons butter or margarine
½ teaspoon salt
pinch of pepper
¾ cup water

Soak the apricots in water overnight. Trim excess fat from the pork fillets and split carefully down the centre, without cutting the fillet in half. Drain the apricots. Peel and slice the apple. Arrange the apricots and apple slices in the centre of the fillet. Draw the edges together and tie securely with string. Melt the butter or margarine in a frying pan and brown the meat on all sides. Season with salt and pepper. Add the water, cover, and simmer for 1 hour or until the meat is tender. Remove the string before serving the meat. Slice the fillets and serve with a gravy made by thickening the meat juices in the frypan.

Note: Stuffed Pork Fillet can also be cooked in a lidded casserole dish in a moderately slow oven for 1-1½ hours or until tender.

CHERRY VEAL

Serves: 4
Oven temperature: moderate

4 thin slices veal
seasoned flour for coating
2 tablespoons butter or margarine
1 can red cherries (about 425 g or 15 oz)
½ cup red wine
½ teaspoon cardamom seeds or 3-4 cardamon pods
2 tablespoons sherry
salt and pepper to taste
¼ cup double cream

Toss veal slices in flour seasoned with salt and pepper. Fry in hot butter or margarine until golden brown on both sides. Remove from pan and place in a shallow casserole dish. Add cherries and their juice to the pan. Then add all other ingredients, except cream, and bring to the boil, scraping up the crusty bits on the bottom of the pan. Tip this sauce over veal. Cover and bake in a moderate oven for 35-40 minutes or till tender. Just before serving stir in the cream. If desired, use 1 cup fresh cherries, adding ½ cup water or orange juice.

HUNGARIAN PORK PAPRIKA

Serves: 3-4
Oven temperature: moderate

750 g (1½ lb) pork fillet
1 teaspoon salt
1 tablespoon plain flour
3 tablespoons butter, margarine or oil
2 onions, chopped
2 ripe tomatoes, peeled and chopped
2 green peppers, sliced
½ teaspoon paprika
pinch salt
1 cup white wine
2 cups sour cream

Cut pork into thin slices then roll in flour and salt. Shake, then fry in butter, margarine or oil until brown on all sides. Remove and place in a wide casserole or saucepan. Add onions, tomatoes and peppers to frying pan and cook until softened. Sprinkle with paprika and salt, add the wine, stir, cook for a few minutes, then pour over the meat. It should cover the meat (add more wine if necessary) — that's why you need a wide casserole. Top with a lid and simmer gently for about 25 minutes, or cook in a moderate oven. Add sour cream to the casserole, stirring to combine. Continue to cook for about another 30 minutes or until meat is tender. Taste for salt.

If the sauce is too thick, thin with a little wine or water. This is good served with dumplings, rice or potatoes, and you can add a few rounds of green peppers and sliced tomatoes to the top of the meat for colour.

Variation: Try this recipe with chicken as well. For Hungarian Chicken Paprika, cut the meat into thick serving pieces, brown in butter, margarine or oil and cook in the sauce just as you would the pork fillet.

PORK CASSEROLE

Serves: 4-6

750 g-1 kg (1½-2 lb) fillet, or lean leg, of
    pork
3 tablespoons lard, butter or margarine
1 onion, chopped
juice of ½ lemon
bay leaf
1½-2 teaspoons salt
freshly ground black pepper
1 cup red wine
4 tablespoons plain flour
½ cup white wine
1 cup water
1 chicken stock cube
¾ cup sliced mushrooms
2 cloves garlic, crushed
2 tablespoons butter or margarine
1 cup sour cream

Slice fillet of pork thinly, or cut leg of pork into cubes. Melt lard, butter or margarine in a large saucepan or flameproof casserole and gently fry onion for 5 minutes. Add pork, lemon juice, bay leaf, salt, pepper and ½ cup red wine, cover and cook gently for 15 minutes. Lift pork out. Add flour to pan and cook over a medium heat, stirring continuously for 1-2 minutes. Add remaining red wine, white wine, water and chicken stock cube and bring to the boil, stirring continuously. Meanwhile, fry mushrooms and crushed garlic in a saucepan in melted butter or margarine for 2-3 minutes. Return pork to pan, add mushroom mixture and simmer, covered, for 15 minutes for fillet pork and 25 minutes for leg pork, or until meat is tender. Taste and adjust seasoning if necessary. Add sour cream and reheat without boiling. Serve hot with creamed potatoes and Spiced Red Cabbage (see page 104).

Note: Pork Casserole can also be cooked in a lidded casserole dish in a moderately slow oven for ½-1 hour or until tender.

STUFFED LOIN OF VEAL

Serves: 6-8
Oven temperature: moderate

1.25 kg (2½ lb) loin of veal
grated rind and juice of 1 lemon
4 mushrooms, chopped
1 cup fine white breadcrumbs
1 tablespoon chopped parsley
1 cup chopped streaky bacon
4 anchovy fillets
salt and pepper
1 egg yolk
milk (optional)
¾ cup butter or margarine
1 cup chicken stock (see page 154) or
    water and chicken stock cube

Ask the butcher to remove bones and skin from the loin. Rub over with the lemon juice. Combine lemon rind mushrooms, and breadcrumbs, together with parsley, bacon, and the mashed anchovy fillets to make stuffing. Season with salt and pepper and moisten with the egg yolk. If not moist enough add a little milk. Spoon stuffing onto underside of veal and roll up. Tie with string, or use skewers to hold it together. Brown well on all sides in a large heavy flameproof casserole in the melted butter or margarine. Pour the stock over. Cover and cook for 1-1¼ hours in a moderate oven until tender. Turn veal several times during cooking and baste with the stock. Serve juices from the pan as a sauce.

PORK WITH APPLES

Serves: 6
Oven temperature: moderate

6 pork leg chops, cut thick
lard, butter or margarine
salt and pepper
¼ teaspoon dried mixed herbs
4 cooking apples, peeled and chopped
    into dice
1 medium onion, finely chopped
1 tablespoon light brown sugar
2 tablespoons dry white wine

The chops should have the rind left on, but make sure there is a minimum of fat between rind and meat, otherwise this dish will end up greasy. Fry the chops on both sides in a frying pan with a little lard, butter or margarine. Use a large, shallow baking dish and place the chops in it flat, in one layer. Where possible press the rinds against the sides of the dish — they'll be crisper that way. Sprinkle with salt, pepper and mixed herbs. Scatter apples and onions over the chops to cover them completely. Sprinkle again lightly with salt and then sugar. Add wine, but be careful not to add too much. Cover lightly with aluminium foil or a lid. Cook in a moderate oven for 1½ hours or until tender. Serve each chop with its own onion and apple topping.

PORK AND PAPRIKA CASSEROLE

Serves: 4
Oven temperature: moderate

750 g (1½ lb) lean pork chump, shoulder
    or neck chops
1 cup thickly sliced onion
½-1 cup sliced mushrooms
¼ cup finely chopped green pepper or
    celery
1-2 tablespoons paprika
2 beef stock cubes
1 cup hot water
arrowroot or cornflour to thicken
chopped parsley

Cut pork into cubes. Mix the pork, onion, mushrooms and green pepper or celery in a deep ovenproof dish. Add the paprika (the larger amount gives a better colour) and stock cubes dissolved in the water. Cover tightly and cook in a moderate oven for 1½ hours for chump chops, a little longer for shoulder or neck meat. Do not overcook. Thicken casserole with a thin arrowroot or cornflour paste. Sprinkle with chopped parsley and serve on buttered rice, or with baked potatoes and a green vegetable.

VEAL DAUBE

Serves: 8-12
Oven temperature: moderately slow

3 kg (6 lb) rump or shoulder veal
125 g (4 oz) ham or bacon
olive oil
1 teaspoon salt
¼ teaspoon allspice
pinch powdered cloves
¼ teaspoon oregano
¼ teaspoon powdered sage
pinch cayenne pepper
pinch black pepper
1 tablespoon plain flour
2 tablespoons dripping
1 onion, peeled and sliced
1 clove garlic, chopped or crushed
2 carrots, scraped and sliced
2 stalks celery, chopped
1 green pepper, chopped
1 small turnip, diced
1 cup water
½ cup white wine
2 teaspoons capers
sprigs of parsley to garnish

With a sharp-pointed knife make small slits all over the veal. Cut the ham or bacon into small pieces and push them into the slits. Rub oil all over the joint. Mix together the salt, spices, herbs, pepper and flour and rub this mixture well into the meat. Heat the dripping in a large frying pan and brown the veal well on all sides. Remove and place in a heavy casserole dish. Add vegetables to the frying pan and cook till softened and golden brown, adding more dripping if necessary. Scrape vegetables out of pan over the meat. Add water and wine to the meat and vegetables. Top with a lid and cook in a moderately slow oven for 2½-3 hours or till tender.

To serve place the veal on a heated platter. Pour a little of the sauce over the meat and sprinkle it with capers. Garnish with sprigs of parsley. Serve the rest of the sauce in a separate sauce boat.

Note: Veal Daube may also be cooked on top of the stove at a very low simmer.

CORDON BLEU VEAL PARCELS

Serves: 6
Oven temperature: moderate

6 veal escalopes
125 g (¼ lb) ham, very thinly sliced
250 g (½ lb) sharp Cheddar cheese,
   thickly sliced
2 tablespoons seasoned flour
1 egg
2 tablespoons milk
soft white breadcrumbs
2 tablespoons olive oil
1 or 2 cloves garlic
1 tablespoon plain flour (for gravy)
¾ cup stock (see page 154) or water
   and stock cube
¾ cup sherry
salt and pepper
lemon and parsley for serving

Using a meat mallet or a rolling pin, flatten the pieces of veal until thin as possible. Cut into serving pieces and place a thin slice of ham on each piece, cover with a thick slice of cheese, and then with another piece of ham. Fold the veal over the top and secure each piece with toothpicks. Coat each parcel of veal with seasoned flour, then dip it in the egg which has been beaten with the milk. Coat each piece with breadcrumbs. Chill for at least 30 minutes.

Heat the oil in a pan and add the garlic, fry gently, then add the veal and brown on all sides. Drain. Place the veal parcels in one large casserole. Add the tablespoon of flour to the oil in the frying pan and stir until it bubbles. Off the heat add the stock and sherry and season to taste with salt and pepper. Stir until combined then bring to the boil and cook for a few minutes to thicken slightly. Pour around the meat in the casserole. Cover and bake in a moderate oven for about 30 minutes, or until the veal is tender, uncovering it for the last 10 minutes of cooking. The baking time will depend on the thickness of the meat. Serve garnished with lemon wedges and parsley sprigs.

TASTY PINEAPPLE SPARERIBS

Serves: 4-6

1.5 kg (3 lb) pork spareribs
1½ cups cider vinegar
1 cup cornflour
2 tablespoons black treacle
2 tablespoons soy sauce
1 cup oil
1 x 425 g (15 oz) tin pineapple pieces
¾ cup water
2 tablespoons sugar
1 green pepper

Cut the spareribs into individual ribs if the butcher hasn't done so. Bring a large saucepan of water to the boil. Add ½ cup vinegar and spareribs and bring back to the boil. Boil for 15 minutes. Drain. Mix together cornflour, black treacle and soy sauce in a mixing bowl and dip spareribs into mixture. Heat oil in a frying pan and fry spareribs until brown. Remove ribs and drain well. Drain pineapple and reserve ¾ cup pineapple juice. Bring this reserved juice to the boil in a clean frying pan with water, sugar and remaining vinegar. Add spareribs, cover and simmer gently for 25 minutes, turning ribs frequently. Add pineapple pieces and green pepper, seeded and cut into thin strips, and cook for a further 5 minutes. Serve hot.

Note: Tasty Pineapple Spareribs can also be cooked in a lidded casserole dish in a moderate oven for 25-35 minutes or until tender.

PORK WITH APPLES AND CIDER

Serves: 4-6
Oven temperature: moderate

1 kg (2 lb) pork fillet, cut into strips
2 tablespoons plain flour
salt and freshly ground pepper
60 g (2 oz) lard
3 cooking apples
2-3 medium onions
12 dessert prunes
½ teaspoon sage
1 tablespoon Calvados or brandy
1 cup apple cider

Rub the pork in flour, salt and pepper. Melt the lard in a large frying pan, add pork, and fry to brown on all sides. When browned remove from the pan. Peel and slice the apples and onions. Arrange half in the base of a greased casserole dish. Halve the prunes and remove stones. Arrange half the prunes on the apples and onions, layer the pork strips on top. Sprinkle with sage, salt and pepper. Cover with the remaining apples, onions and prunes. Pour over the combined liquor and cider. Cover with a lid and cook in a moderate oven for 2-2½ hours. Check the level of the liquid after about 1½ hours and, if necessary, add a little more cider.

CURRIED PORK SAUSAGES

Serves: 4

750 g (1½ lb) pork sausages
2 tablespoons dripping
1 large onion, chopped
1 clove garlic, chopped
1 tablespoon curry powder
1 tablespoon plain flour
½ cup sliced celery
1 carrot, chopped
1 tomato, skinned and chopped
1 cup sliced green beans
½ pint beef stock (see page 154)
salt

Parboil sausages by placing them in cold water in a saucepan and bringing them to simmering point. Remove from heat and leave standing in water for 10 minutes, then cut sausages into chunky slices. Heat dripping in a deep pan and brown sausage slices on all sides. Lift out and keep aside. Fry onion and garlic in same pan for 10 minutes, stir in curry powder and flour and cook for a further 5 minutes. Add remaining vegetables, stock and salt to taste, stirring well. Bring to simmering point, cover, and cook for 15 minutes. Add sausage slices and simmer, covered, for a further 15-20 minutes. Serve with boiled rice and a fruit chutney.

VEAL GOULASH

Serves: 6

1 kg (2 lb) veal shoulder
3 teaspoons paprika
2 teaspoons salt
¼ teaspoon pepper
2 tablespoons cornflour
2 tablespoons oil
2 large onions, chopped
1 teaspoon sugar
2 large tomatoes, skinned and chopped
½ teaspoon chilli powder
½ teaspoon caraway seeds (optional)
bouquet garni (see page 82)
1 large red pepper
monosodium glutamate

Cut veal into cubes. In a clean paper bag mix paprika, salt, pepper and cornflour, add veal and shake until coated with seasoned flour. Heat oil in a large saucepan, fry veal until browned, cooking in two or three lots, then remove. Add onions, sprinkle with sugar, fry gently till golden brown. Add tomatoes, chilli powder and caraway seeds. Stir in meat and add bouquet garni. Cover and simmer gently over a low heat until cooked, about 2 hours. Add chopped, seeded red pepper and a pinch of monosodium glutamate during last 30 minutes of cooking. Remove bouquet garni. Taste and adjust seasoning, if necessary, before serving.

Note: The tomatoes usually supply sufficient liquid for cooking, but if necessary a little water may be added — not too much. Veal Goulash can also be cooked in a lidded casserole dish in a moderately slow oven for 1½-2 hours or until tender.

VEAL ROLLS WITH CIDER

Serves: 6-8

Stuffing
125 g (4 oz) small mushrooms
2 tablespoons butter or margarine
½ onion, finely chopped
2 tablespoons dry breadcrumbs
1 tablespoon parsley, chopped
1 cup cooked chicken, cut into small
    pieces
1 egg
¼ cup medium sweet cider
salt and pepper to taste

Veal
6-8 veal steaks, thinly sliced
2 tablespoons plain flour
1 teaspoon salt
pinch pepper
1 egg
4 tablespoons butter or margarine
1 cup medium sweet cider
1 chicken stock cube
2 teaspoons cornflour
1 tablespoon cold water

To make stuffing: Reserve a few mushrooms for garnishing and chop the rest. Melt 2 tablespoons of the butter or margarine in a pan, add onion and fry gently till softened. Add mushrooms and fry further till they are softened. Remove from heat and add crumbs, parsley, diced chicken and 1 egg. Mix well, adding a few tablespoons of cider to make the mixture spreadable. Add salt and pepper to taste.

To prepare veal: With a meat mallet flatten veal steaks until thin. Cut each one in half. Spread a spoonful of filling over each piece of veal. Roll up and secure with a toothpick. Mix together flour, salt and pepper. Beat egg and dip veal rolls in it and then toss rolls in seasoned flour to coat lightly. Fry in the remaining 4 tablespoons butter or margarine until golden brown on all sides. Pour in the cider and sprinkle with the crumbled stock cube. Bring to the boil. Cover with a lid and simmer till tender, about 25-35 minutes.

Remove rolls to a serving platter and keep warm. Slice reserved mushrooms, add to cooking liquid and boil for a few minutes. Mix cornflour with a little cold water to make a thin paste. Add to the cooking juices. Bring to the boil and cook till thickened. Pour over veal rolls. Serve with mashed or scalloped potatoes, buttered rice or noodles.

Note: Veal Rolls with Cider may also be cooked in a lidded casserole dish in a moderately slow oven for 35-45 minutes or until tender.

VEAL WITH MUSHROOMS

Serves: 4

**750 g (1½ lb) veal shoulder or breast,
 boned**
3 tablespoons butter or margarine
2 tablespoons plain flour
**2½ cups veal or chicken stock (see page
 154) or water and chicken stock cube
 cube**
salt and pepper
8 button onions
8 button mushrooms
1 egg yolk
2 tablespoons double cream
few drops of lemon juice
chopped parsley for garnish

Cut veal into cubes and fry slowly in the butter or margarine without colouring. Stir in the flour and cook over a low heat for 5 minutes. Add stock slowly, stirring continuously, and bring to the boil. Season lightly, cover, and simmer gently for 30 minutes. Add onions and simmer for 15 minutes, then add mushrooms and cook a further 15 minutes, or until vegetables are tender. Mix egg yolk with cream and stir into veal and vegetables over a low heat (or, preferably, shake the pan gently till thoroughly mixed). Do not boil. Stir in lemon juice and serve sprinkled with chopped parsley.

PORK AND ORANGE CASSEROLE

Serves: 6-8

1 kg (2 lb) pork tenderloin
1 tablespoon butter or margarine
½ cup chopped onion
1 teaspoon grated orange rind
⅓ cup orange juice
⅔ cup dry sherry
1 tablespoon sugar
2 teaspoons salt, or to taste
dash pepper
1 bay leaf
1 tablespoon cornflour
1 tablespoon cold water

Trim any pieces of fat from the pork. Heat the butter or margarine in a pan and brown the tenderloin on all sides. Remove from the pan. In the same pan cook the onion or shallot until tender, then add the orange rind and juice, sherry, sugar, salt, pepper and bay leaf. Return the meat to the pan. Cover and simmer for 1 hour, or until tender, turning occasionally.

Remove the meat to a hot serving dish and cut into thin slices. Blend the cornflour with the water, stir into the orange flavoured gravy in the pan, bring to the boil and cook for 1 or 2 minutes. Spoon some of the gravy over the sliced pork and serve the remainder separately.

Note: Pork and Orange Casserole can also be cooked in a lidded casserole dish in a moderately slow oven for 1-1½ hours or until tender.

PORK PARISIENNE

Serves: 3-4
Oven temperature: moderate

500 g (1 lb) pork chops
1 onion
1 tablespoon oil, butter or margarine
2 large chopped tomatoes
½ cup claret
vegetable stock
½ cup rolled oats
garlic salt
**1 x 450 g (15½ oz) can condensed pea
 and ham soup**

Bone the chops and cut the meat into chunks. Lightly brown meat and sliced onion in 1 tablespoon oil, butter or margarine. Place meat and onion in a casserole dish with the cut up tomatoes. Gently pour in the claret. Fill the casserole with the vegetable stock to the level of the meat. Sprinkle with the oatmeal and add garlic salt to taste. Gently stir the pea and ham soup into the mixture, cover and cook for 1 hour in a moderate oven, or until tender, and serve hot with french beans.

ROAST STUFFED BREAST OF VEAL

Serves: 8-10
Oven temperature: moderate

Stuffing
500 g (1 lb) sausage meat
½ teaspoon mixed herbs
1 egg
1 onion, finely chopped
salt and pepper

Veal
1 x 1.5 kg (3 lb) breast of veal
2 tablespoons lard, butter or margarine
1 large onion, sliced
1 large carrot, sliced
2½ cups chicken stock (see page 154) or
water and chicken stock cubes
1 tablespoon cornflour

Ask your butcher to bone the breast of veal and cut a pocket in the middle.

To make the stuffing: Mix sausage meat, herbs, egg, finely chopped onion and salt and pepper together.

To prepare veal: Push stuffing in pocket of veal, roll up joint and tie securely. Grease a roasting pan with melted lard, butter or margarine and fry sliced onion and carrot until golden. Place meat on top of vegetables and brush with lard. Brown the meat in a moderate oven for 30 minutes. When well coloured, add stock and cook for a further 1½ hours, basting every 30 minutes. When cooked remove meat from the roasting pan to serving dish and keep warm. Skim fat from stock, add cornflour blended with a little cold water to pan gravy and bring to the boil, stirring continuously. Season to taste with more salt and pepper if necessary. Serve sauce poured over veal.

Variation: Grated rind 1 lemon may be added to the stuffing or 2 tablespoons sultanas, if desired.

COFFEE VEAL

Serves: 4-6
Oven temperature: moderate

2 tablespoons oil
30 g (1 oz) butter or margarine
1 kg (2 lb) veal fillet, cut into cubes and
coated with plain flour
salt and freshly ground pepper
2 tablespoons chopped spring onions
1½ cups chicken stock (see page 154)
1 cup brewed coffee
1 tablespoon Tia Maria, or brandy
125 g (4 oz) baby mushrooms, or use
canned champignons, drained
1 tablespoon butter or margarine
1 tablespoon plain flour
½ cup double cream

Heat oil with butter or margarine in a large frying pan. Add the veal and sprinkle with the salt and pepper. Fry until the veal is browned on all sides. Add the spring onions and fry for a few minutes. Pour in the chicken stock and coffee and bring to the boil, stirring all the time. Add the Tia Maria or brandy, and mushrooms. Cover with a lid and simmer over a low flame or in a moderate oven for 1-1½ hours or until veal is tender. Blend the butter or margarine with the flour. Gradually stir this mixture into the veal and heat through. Add the cream and stir well. Serve with buttered rice sprinkled with parsley.

VEAL PROVENCAL

Serves: 6-8

1-1½ kg (2-3 lb) piece of veal
2 cloves garlic
salt and pepper
2 tablespoons oil
12 small tomatoes
12 small onions
2 shallots, chopped
small branch fresh rosemary or 1
 teaspoon dried rosemary
salt and pepper

Cut slits in the veal and push slivers of garlic into them. Rub the joint all over with salt and pepper. Heat oil in a large saucepan and brown the veal on all sides. Turn down the flame and add whole tomatoes, peeled if desired. Then add whole onions, chopped shallots, chopped fresh rosemary, or dried, salt and pepper to taste. Cover and cook very gently until the veal is tender, about 2 hours. The dish generally needs no liquid — there should be enough in the tomatoes. Serve veal on a bed of onions with the tomatoes all around, with a crisp green salad and crunchy hot bread with lashings of butter.

Note: Veal Provençal can also be cooked in a lidded casserole dish in a moderately slow oven for 1½-2 hours or until tender.

OSSO BUCCO

Serves: 4
Oven temperature: moderately slow

4 shins of veal
1 onion, chopped
2 stalks celery, chopped
4 tablespoons diced bacon
2 tablespoons butter or margarine
½ cup dry white wine
pinch of thyme
1 bay leaf
2 cloves garlic, crushed
500 g (1 lb) ripe tomatoes, skinned,
 seeded and chopped
4 tablespoons plain flour
salt and pepper
1 tablespoon oil
stock or water
grated rind of ½ lemon
chopped parsley for garnish

Ask the butcher to cut veal shins into 5 cm (2 inch) pieces, across the leg bone. Fry the onion, celery and bacon in butter or margarine, add wine, thyme and bay leaf, and cook slowly for 20 minutes. Add garlic and tomatoes and cook for a further 5 minutes. Roll veal in mixture of salt, pepper and flour and in a clean frying pan fry in oil until light brown. Place fried veal in an ovenproof casserole and add cooked vegetables and stock or water to cover. Cook in a moderately slow oven for 1½ hours. Just before serving add lemon rind. Sprinkle with chopped parsley and serve with rice pilaff or saffron rice.

PINEAPPLE PORK

Serves: 5-6
Oven temperature: moderate

5-6 thick pork chops
3 tablespoons plain flour
2 chicken stock cubes
2 tablespoons brown sugar
2 tablespoons brandy
½ cup cider
1 small can pineapple pieces (425 g or 15
 oz)
1 large onion, roughly chopped
1 green pepper, roughly chopped

Rub pork chops with the flour and arrange side by side in a casserole dish. Combine chicken stock cubes and brown sugar with the brandy in a bowl, add the remaining ingredients and spoon over the chops. Cover and bake in a moderate oven for 1 hour or until tender. Serve with fried potatoes.

VEAL BLANQUETTE

Serves: 6
Oven temperature: moderately slow

12 veal escalopes
2 tablespoons butter or margarine
½ tablespoon oil
¼ cup chopped spring onions
1 cup dry white wine
1 cup beef stock (see page 154) water
    and stock cubes, or beef consommé
3 teaspoons chopped tarragon, fresh
    or dried
2 teaspoons cornflour
1 tablespoon water
salt and pepper
2 tablespoons softened butter, or
    double cream

Flatten veal escalopes, then dry well with paper towels. Heat butter or margarine and oil in a frying pan and when foam subsides add veal, 3-4 pieces at a time. Cook till lightly browned. Remove and place in a casserole dish. Add spring onions to pan and fry for a minute, then pour in wine and stock and add tarragon. Simmer until liquid has boiled down to about 1 cup. Mix cornflour to a cream with 1 tablespoon cold water. Slowly add to simmering sauce until thickened. Add salt and pepper to taste. Pour sauce over the veal and cover dish with a piece of greaseproof paper, then with a lid. Place in a moderately slow oven and cook for 20-25 minutes or until tender. Just before serving tilt the pan and swirl the softened butter or cream into the sauce. More tarragon may be added just before serving.

Variation: Sliced baby mushrooms are a good addition. Fry 125 g (4 oz) mushrooms in butter in a separate pan and arrange around the serving plate as a garnish.

Note: This dish also freezes well. A little more wine may be needed after thawing, before reheating.

VEAL BIRDS

Serves: 4-6
Oven temperature: moderately slow

Stuffing
2 cups soft breadcrumbs
¼ cup finely chopped suet
1 tablespoon chopped parsley
1 teaspoon thyme or mixed herbs
½ teaspoon grated lemon rind
½ teaspoon salt
¼ teaspoon pepper
1 egg, beaten

Veal Birds
6 very thin slices veal, from fillet or leg
4 tablespoons butter or margarine
1 onion, chopped
3 tablespoons plain flour
2 cups chicken stock (see page 154) or
    water and chicken stock cube
salt and pepper

To prepare stuffing: Combine all the stuffing ingredients and mix thoroughly.

To prepare Veal Birds: Divide stuffing into 6 portions and spread on each slice of veal. Roll up and secure with cotton or cocktail sticks. Heat the butter or margarine in a frying pan and brown the meat rolls. Place the rolls in an ovenproof casserole. Fry the onion in the butter until soft, stir in the flour and cook for 1 minute. Add half the stock and heat until thickened, stirring constantly. Add the remaining liquid and stir until boiling. Season to taste with salt and pepper. Pour the sauce over the veal rolls, cover and cook in a moderately slow oven for 1¼ hours or until the meat is tender. Remove the cotton or cocktail sticks before serving.

I'm game if you are

Game and casseroles were made for each other.
The marriage of tough, sinewy, muscle-bound
meat with soft and gentle cooking makes a
perfect meal. But, like many beautiful
romances, game cooking takes time to develop.
Some recipes call for soaking in a marinade for
days on end to help break down the gristly
sinews, then quite a few hours for the cooking.
But, like true love, it's worth it.

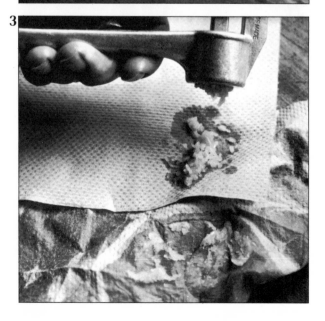

GARLIC

1 *Peeling garlic.* Before you peel a clove of garlic squash it firmly with the flat blade of a knife. You'll find the garlic clove much easier to peel after squashing — the garlic just slips out of the skin.

2 *Crushing garlic without a garlic crusher.* You don't need a garlic crusher to crush garlic to a cream, all you need is salt and a round-ended knife.

Pile a teaspoon of salt on the corner of a chopping board. Place the peeled garlic clove on the salt then scrape it firmly into the salt, pressing your finger down on the end of the knife. Mix the garlic with the salt and squash it well into the board. In seconds you'll have a smooth garlic cream.

Remove garlic smell from board and fingers by rubbing with salt and then washing under *cold* water. Hot water just fixes the smell in for good.

3 *No returns garlic.* If you love the taste of garlic, but can't cope with the after effects, try this little trick. It is the oil that oozes out of your pores and hangs on your breath, so the solution is to remove it.

Just crush garlic onto kitchen paper, then wrap it up in the paper and squeeze firmly. Scrape the garlic fibres off the paper into the food. Because most of the garlic flavour is squashed into the paper use more cloves with this method than you would normally.

Apricot Rabbit (page 79)

MARINATED VENISON

Serves: allow 250 g (8 oz) per person
Oven temperature: moderate

Marinade
2 cups red wine
½ cup oil
½ cup wine vinegar
1 teaspoon salt
1 bay leaf
1 clove garlic, crushed
2 juniper berries
1 onion, sliced

Venison
haunch or saddle of venison
1 tablespoon sugar
½ teaspoon ground ginger
bacon rashers to cover
1 tablespoon butter or margarine
1 tablespoon plain flour
1 tablespoon redcurrant jelly

To prepare marinade: Mix all ingredients together.

To prepare venison: Trim and wipe venison and place in a large bowl. Pour marinade over meat and allow to stand for at least 24 hours. Turn several times to keep meat under liquid during this time. Lift out and pat dry when ready to cook.

Place venison in a casserole dish or roasting pan and rub over with the sugar and ginger mixed together. Criss-cross bacon over the top of the meat. Pour strained marinade around meat and cover with a lid or foil. Cook in a moderate oven. Allow to cook for 30 minutes per 500 g (1 lb) and 30 minutes extra. Remove venison to a heated serving dish and keep hot. Mix together the flour and butter or margarine, and add to the gravy in the pan, stirring continuously. Stir in redcurrant jelly. Serve gravy with roast venison.

RABBIT WITH CIDER AND PRUNES

Serves: 4-6

10-12 prunes
1 cup medium sweet cider
1 large or 2 small rabbits
4 tablespoons bacon fat
3 tablespoons brandy
4 small white onions, quartered
2 tablespoons plain flour
1½ cups medium sweet cider
2-3 cloves
bouquet garni (see page 82)
salt and pepper
1 teaspoon brown sugar

Put prunes to soak in 1 cup cider while cooking the rabbit. Cut rabbits into joints, removing legs and cutting back into 3 or 4 pieces. Brown the joints in half the bacon fat. When rabbit is brown, add brandy and set alight, being careful to turn your face away as it flares. Shake pan till flames subside. Remove rabbit pieces. Add remaining bacon fat and quartered onions and brown slightly. Sprinkle in flour, stir and fry till golden brown. Off the heat add the 1½ cups cider. Stir till blended and then bring to the boil, stirring. Add cloves, tied in a muslin bag, bouquet garni, salt and pepper and brown sugar. Cover with a lid and simmer gently over a low heat for 40-45 minutes. Add soaked prunes and simmer a further 30 minutes longer. Remove cloves and bouquet and serve with boiled potatoes and glazed carrots.

Note: Rabbit with Cider and Prunes may also be cooked in a lidded casserole dish in a moderately slow oven for 1½-2 hours.

Spanish Chicken Livers (page 86)

VENISON ROLLS

Serves: 6

Filling
**125 g (4 oz) venison scraps or minced
  beef**
1 small onion, finely chopped
1 tablespoon oil
125 g (4 oz) mushrooms, finely chopped
2 tablespoons fine breadcrumbs
salt and pepper

Venison
6 thin slices venison steak
3 rashers fat bacon
1 tablespoon plain flour
½ cup red wine
**1 cup beef stock (see page 154) or water
  and stock cube**
salt and pepper
**1 tablespoon cranberry or other tart-
  flavoured jelly**

To make the filling: Mince scraps of venison or, if not available, use minced beef. Put in a bowl. Fry onion in oil until soft and golden. Add mushrooms and cook for 1 minute. Add cooked mixture to the meat and stir in the breadcrumbs. Season lightly.

To prepare Venison Rolls: Beat venison steak until about 5 mm (¼ inch) thick. Remove rind from bacon and cut each rasher in half.

Spread a little stuffing on each piece of venison and roll up. Wrap in the bacon strip and secure with either toothpicks or string. Place rolls side by side in a heavy-based casserole and cook over high heat. Turn once and brown other side. Sprinkle flour over meat and add wine and stock, salt and pepper. Bring to boil, then lower the heat and cover. Simmer for 1 hour or until meat is tender. Lift out rolls and remove toothpicks or string. Keep rolls hot. Stir jelly into sauce and pour over Venison Rolls. Serve with rice.

Note: Venison Rolls can also be cooked in a lidded casserole dish in a moderately slow oven for 1-1½ hours.

PIGEONS AND PEAS IN RED WINE

Serves: 6

12 small pigeons
**1½ cups chicken stock (see page 154) or
  water and chicken stock cubes**
½ bottle (13 fluid oz) red wine
250 g (8 oz) butter or margarine
½ cup brandy
¾ cup diced, lean, thick rashers bacon
¼ cup plain flour
salt and pepper
bouquet garni (see page 82)
250 g (8 oz) fresh peas

Remove pigeon livers, gizzards, etc. and chop them finely. Place in an electric blender with chicken stock and wine and blend thoroughly. Melt butter or margarine in a heavy saucepan and brown birds thoroughly. Flame in the brandy. Remove pigeons and add bacon. Brown and remove. Stir in flour and cook lightly for 1 minute over a low heat. Add chicken stock and wine mixture, salt and pepper and bouquet garni and simmer for 5 minutes. Add the birds, bacon and peas. Cook a further 30-45 minutes or until birds are tender. Serve hot with a red wine to drink with it.

Note: Pigeons and Peas in Red Wine may also be cooked in a lidded casserole dish in a moderately slow oven for ¾-1 hour or until tender.

GAMEKEEPER'S MARINADE

2 cups red wine
1 cup wine vinegar
1 cup oil
½ cup chopped celery
½ cup chopped onion
½ cup chopped carrots
handful freshly chopped herbs (thyme,
    rosemary and/or marjoram) or use 2
    teaspoons dried herbs
2 tablespoons crushed juniper berries
1 clove crushed garlic
4 bay leaves

Mix all ingredients together and pour over meat in an earthenware, plastic or stainless steel container. Soak the meat in the marinade for 3-4 days to tenderise and add flavour. Leave out of the fridge for the first day so the wine and herbs penetrate the meat. This marinade can be used for any game meat. It can also be used with pieces of beef or lamb to give them extra flavour.

RABBIT WITH PRUNES AND PINE NUTS

Serves: 4-6
Oven temperature: moderately slow

2 small rabbits
¼ cup olive oil
2 onions, chopped
4 tomatoes, skinned and chopped
1 bay leaf
2 cloves garlic, crushed
30 peeled, toasted almonds
sprigs of parsley
½ cup water
salt
⅓ cup pine nuts
20 prunes

Wash and dry rabbits and cut into serving pieces. Heat oil in a flameproof casserole or large heavy saucepan. Fry onions slowly until golden, add tomatoes and bay leaf and continue frying for 5 minutes. When mixture has combined add rabbit and simmer, covered, for 30-45 minutes; or transfer into a casserole dish, cover and cook in a moderately slow oven for ¾ hour.

Crush garlic, almonds and parsley with a mortar and pestle and mix in water, or blend all together in an electric blender. Add ground mixture to rabbit, salt to taste and continue cooking for 30 minutes or until tender. Simmer pine nuts and prunes in water in separate saucepans. The pine nuts will require 10-15 minutes. Cooking time of prunes varies according to size. Drain and add pine nuts and prunes to rabbit just before serving.

Variation: Instead of pine nuts, walnuts or almonds may be used.

Note: If added before the end of cooking, the pine nuts will not remain white and the prunes may over sweeten the sauce. I have cooked the dish with them added from the beginning and it's still delicious.

VENISON STEW

Serves: 4

500 g (1 lb) venison
2 onions, sliced
3 tablespoons olive oil
1 rasher fat bacon, chopped
1 bay leaf
6 peppercorns
2 teaspoons tomato paste
2 cups water
small sprig of rosemary
1 clove garlic, crushed
½ cup dry red wine
salt and pepper

Cut venison into cubes. Fry onions in hot oil in a large saucepan. When soft add bacon and fry. Add meat, bay leaf and peppercorns and cook for 2-3 minutes until meat is lightly browned. Add tomato paste, water, rosemary, garlic and wine to meat mixture and season to taste with salt and pepper. Bring to the boil, reduce heat and simmer, covered, for 2 hours, stirring occasionally and adding more water if necessary. Test tenderness of meat by piercing with a fork. Check seasoning and add more salt and pepper if necessary before serving.

Note: Venison Stew may also be cooked in a lidded casserole dish in a moderately slow oven for 1½-2 hours or until tender.

JUGGED HARE

Serves: 4-6

1 hare, preferably freshly killed
2 tablespoons brandy
2 tablespoons olive oil
salt and pepper
1 onion, thinly sliced
dry red wine
250 g (8 oz) bacon
125-250 g (4-8 oz) butter or margarine
20 small white onions
2 tablespoons plain flour
bouquet garni (see page 82)
20 mushrooms
croûtons

If possible obtain a fresh hare and save the blood and the liver. Cut hare into serving pieces and place in bowl with brandy, oil, a little salt and pepper and the onion. Cover with dry red wine. Allow to stand in a cool place for several hours, preferably overnight.

Cut bacon into squares and cook in butter in a large heavy saucepan. Use the maximum amount of butter for best results, but the quantity can be reduced to 125 g (4 oz). Drain the bacon as soon as it browns and put to one side. Fry the onions in the butter and bacon fat mixture, sprinkle with flour, stir and cook until lightly browned. Drain the hare, add the pieces to the onions and fat and brown well. Add sufficient of the wine marinade to cover. Add bouquet garni, cover pan and allow to cook gently over low to moderate heat for 40-45 minutes. Add mushrooms and simmer a further 5 minutes. Remove hare to a deep warm serving dish. Spoon mushrooms, reserved bacon and onions around the hare. Stir reserved blood and chopped liver into the sauce and cook for 2-3 minutes. Strain sauce over the hare and vegetables. Serve garnished with croûtons.

Note: Jugged Hare may also be cooked in a lidded casserole dish in a moderately slow oven for ¾-1 hour.

BRAISED HARE

Serves: 4-5

1 young hare
2 tablespoons lemon juice
freshly ground black pepper
2 rashers fat bacon
1 onion, sliced
1 carrot, sliced
2 stalks celery, sliced
4 tablespoons butter or margarine
½ cup red wine
salt
1 sprig parsley
1 sprig thyme
1 bay leaf

Cut hare into serving portions and rub with lemon juice and freshly ground black pepper. Wrap in pieces of fat bacon and allow to stand in a dish for several hours. Fry the onion, carrot and celery lightly in hot butter or margarine. Scrape the vegetables into a flameproof casserole. Pour in the wine and season with salt. Tie parsley, thyme and bay leaf together to make a bouquet garni and place on vegetables. Put the bacon wrapped pieces of hare on the bed of vegetables. Place lid on casserole. Cook gently for about 1½ hours or until meat is tender. The cooking liquid may be thickened with a beurre manie if desired (see page 157).

Note: Braised Hare may also be cooked in a lidded casserole dish in a moderately slow oven for 1½-2 hours or until tender.

HARE WITH SOUR CREAM SAUCE

Serves: 6
Oven temperature: moderately slow

1 saddle of hare, larded with strips of
    pork fat
1 teaspoon salt
1 teaspoon paprika
plain flour
125 g (4 oz) butter or margarine
2 cups sour cream
½ cup beef stock (see page 154) or water
    and beef stock cube
¼ cup vinegar
1 bay leaf
½ teaspoon dried thyme
juice of ½ lemon
1 tablespoon capers
1 tablespoon beurre manié (see page 157)

Rub the larded saddle of hare with salt and paprika and sprinkle it generously with flour. Brown on all sides in heated butter or margarine in a frying pan. Transfer to a casserole dish. Heat sour cream, beef stock and vinegar together and pour over hare. Add bay leaf and thyme. Cover and roast in a moderately slow oven for approximately 1-1½ hours, depending on age of hare. Baste every so often. Remove hare and keep warm. Strain pan juices and add lemon juice and capers. Stir in 1 tablespoon of beurre manié to thicken. Bring mixture to a boil and serve in a separate sauce boat with roast hare.

PHEASANT ESPAGNOLE

Serves: 4

2 x 1 kg (2 lb) pheasants
¼ cup olive oil
1½ cups port wine
salt
4 tablespoons butter or margarine
3 shallots, finely chopped
60 g (2 oz) pâté de foie gras
¼ cup brandy
¼ cup dry sherry
2 teaspoons salt
pinch of black pepper
4 chicken livers and 2 pheasant livers,
    finely chopped

Marinate the cleaned pheasants overnight in oil and port wine, drain them and reserve marinade. Place pheasants in a shallow roasting pan and sprinkle them with salt. Brush with half the melted butter or margarine. Roast pheasants in a hot oven for 15 minutes. Remove birds from roasting pan. Remove drumsticks and cut breast meat and any other meat in strips about 1 cm (½ inch) wide. Melt remaining butter or margarine in frying pan, add the shallots and cook till softened. Add the pâté de foie gras, brandy and sherry. Set alight (watch it, it flares) let flames die down then add the wine marinade, salt, pepper and pheasant breast meat and drumsticks and simmer for 30-45 minutes or until meat is cooked (it may need longer). Remove pan from heat and allow to cool slightly for a few minutes. Stir in the chopped chicken and pheasant livers, reheat and simmer for 5 minutes. Adjust seasoning if necessary before serving.

Note: Pheasant Espagnole may also be cooked in a lidded casserole dish in a moderately slow oven for ¾-1 hour or until tender. This recipe may be prepared ahead of time and reheated.

VENISON IN RED WINE

Serves: 4-6

2 kg (4 lb) venison
dry red wine
bouquet garni (see page 82)
4 onions, sliced
185 g (6 oz) butter or margarine
salt and pepper
20 small white onions
1 cup dry white wine
250 g (8 oz) mushrooms (optional)
chopped parsley for garnish

Cut the venison into cubes and place in an earthenware or stainless steel bowl. Cover with dry red wine and add bouquet garni. Leave in a cool place for at least 24 hours.

When ready to cook, drain the venison, reserving the marinade. Fry sliced onions in 4 tablespoons butter or margarine in a flameproof casserole or a large saucepan until golden. Add venison and fry till browned, cooking the meat in a few lots. Return all meat to pan and pour in the reserved marinade. Season to taste with salt and pepper. Allow to come to boil, cover and lower heat to a gentle simmer and cook until meat is tender. This will depend on the age of the venison, about 1¼-2 hours. Fry the small white onions in remaining butter until they begin to soften, but do not allow to colour. Pour over dry white wine and allow onions to poach gently, turning once or twice, until cooked. Add to meat just before serving. If desired, add mushrooms 5 minutes before serving. Serve sprinkled with chopped parsley.

Note: Venison in Red Wine may also be cooked in a lidded casserole dish in a moderately slow oven for 1½-2 hours or until tender.

BRAISED GAME BIRDS

Serves: 3-4
Oven temperature: moderately slow

1 wild duck or pheasant
1 rasher bacon, finely chopped
1 onion, finely chopped
2 tablespoons butter or margarine
1 tablespoon plain flour
2 cups chicken stock (see page 154) or
   water and chicken stock cubes
2 tablespoons white wine
salt and pepper
¼ cup orange juice or redcurrant jelly
10 soaked dried apricots or 10 button
   mushrooms

Place the cleaned bird in a roasting pan and cook in a moderately slow oven for 20 minutes. Remove and cut into small serving pieces. Fry the bacon and onion in hot butter or margarine in a large heavy saucepan, sprinkle with flour and cook for a few minutes. Off the heat add the stock and wine and stir until combined, then bring to boil. Season with salt and pepper and if cooking wild duck add the orange juice, if pheasant, add the redcurrant jelly.

Place the pieces of bird in the sauce and simmer gently until tender, about 45 minutes. Add the apricots to the duck, or the mushrooms to the pheasant, 10 minutes before serving, and cook gently. Arrange braised bird with apricots or mushrooms on a hot plate and boil the sauce rapidly to reduce it by about half the quantity. Pour over braised birds.

Note: Braised Game Birds may also be cooked in a lidded casserole dish in a moderately slow oven for ¾-1 hour or until tender.

APRICOT RABBIT

Serves: 6-10
Oven temperature: moderate

4 tablespoons olive oil
1 clove garlic, chopped
10 baby onions
1 x 1-2 kg (2-4 lb) rabbit, jointed
1 can apricot halves (about 840 g or 30
   oz)
salt and pepper
½ cup tomato paste
½ cup chicken stock (see page 154) or
   water and stock cubes
½ cup dry vermouth or sherry
½ cup raisins
¼ cup pine nuts
bunch parsley

Heat the oil, add garlic, onions and rabbit pieces and fry until browned. Strain the apricot syrup into the pan, reserving the fruit. Add all other ingredients, stir well, then cover with a lid and either gently simmer, or bake in a moderate oven for about 1 hour or until rabbit is tender. Add apricot halves 10 minutes before end of cooking. Remove rabbit to a hot plate and if sauce is too thin, boil down a little. Pour over rabbit.

Serve with a risotto or buttery noodles and with cranberry sauce in a separate sauce boat.

RABBIT WITH ONIONS AND WINE

Serves: 6-8

**1 kg (2 lb) onions, peeled and finely
  sliced**
3 tablespoons olive oil
1 kg (2 lb) rabbit pieces
¾ cup white wine
salt and pepper

Cook the onions in two tablespoons of the oil over a
gentle heat, stirring frequently for about 30 minutes until
softened, but not brown. In a separate pan, fry the rabbit
pieces in the rest of the oil, over a moderate heat, until
they are golden brown and almost cooked. Mix together
the onions and rabbit, add the white wine, salt and
pepper and bring slowly to the boil with the lid on.
Simmer very gently, uncovered, until cooked — about 30-
45 minutes.

Note: Rabbit with Onions and Wine may also be cooked
in a lidded casserole dish in a moderately slow oven for
¾-1 hour.

RABBIT WITH TARRAGON

Serves: 4-6

1 young rabbit, about 1.5 kg (3 lb)
seasoned flour
125 g (4 oz) butter or margarine
¾ cup dry white wine
**2 tablespoons fresh tarragon or 1
  teaspoon dried tarragon**
¼ cup dry white wine

Skin and clean rabbit, reserving the liver if desired. Cut
into serving pieces and sprinkle lightly with a little
seasoned flour. Melt butter or margarine in a large frying
pan and brown the pieces of rabbit quickly on all sides,
being careful not to let the fat burn. Lower the heat, add ¾
cup white wine and cover the pan. Simmer the rabbit
gently for about 45 minutes, or until it is tender.

Soak fresh tarragon leaves or dried tarragon in ¼ cup
wine for 30 minutes. Add the flavoured wine to the frying
pan, raise the heat, and turn the pieces of rabbit over.
Cook for 5 minutes. Remove rabbit to a heated platter and
pour sauce over it. The liver may be fried in butter or
margarine for 5 minutes, chopped and added to the sauce
just before serving.

Note: Rabbit with Tarragon may also be cooked in a
lidded casserole dish in a moderately slow oven for ¾-1
hour.

Getting to the heart of the matter

To many people, 'offal' is a dirty word. Ugh, hate the stuff, is a common reaction — but they don't know what they're missing. Not only does offal taste great — it's good for you too. Look at the food value of most offal and they're right at the top of the vitamin and mineral scale. Such knowledge hasn't always been the case. When I was a child my mother was told that kidneys had no food value at all. Luckily for me she took no notice of the experts and served them up anyway. Her attitude was that anything tasting so delicious just had to be nutritious as well.

What is offal? Well, it's liver, kidney, brains, head, tongue, heart, tripe and trotters — the parts of animals that butchers once threw away. But, judging by the prices of offal these days, people are twigging to its value and flavour.

There are two schools of thought on cooking offal. The French like it cooked quickly. Flash-cooked, and still delicately pink in the middle. The English, on the other hand, believe in cooking offal for hours on end. There are points on both sides, but for casserole cooking I think the latter method is best. Overcooking will produce tough, rubbery meat, but slow, gentle cooking will give a soft, melting texture to all offal, be it brains or heart.

1

2

A BOUQUET GARNI

A bouquet garni is a bunch of fresh mixed herbs often used in casserole cooking. The herbs are wrapped in a small piece of muslin or cloth so that they are easily removed at the end of cooking.

Use a sprig of parsley leaves or stalks, a leafy celery top, a few peppercorns, 1-2 bayleaves and a spray of thyme. Wrap these in the square of cloth and tie the corners together with white string as brown string flavours the dish.

When making a fish casserole I add 1-2 strips of lemon peel to the bouquet for a spicy sour taste.

If fresh herbs are not available then use dried ones and just add a pinch of each of the herbs mentioned above straight into the pot.

FREEZING CASSEROLES

Most casseroles freeze well for a short period. The faster you freeze the dish the more flavour is retained. It's a good idea to put the food into a large plastic freezer bag inside a casserole dish before freezing. When solid remove the bag and its frozen contents, seal thoroughly and label. Then, when needed, all you do is to remove the food from the plastic bag and thaw and heat the casserole in the original dish.

- Don't overcook the casserole. Freezing has a tenderising effect and can make overcooked meat and vegetables go mushy when thawed.

- Remember to remove as much air from the bag as possible before freezing. There are vacuum pumps especially designed for the job, or you can use a drinking straw.

- Use strong plastic bags or airtight containers. Remember, liquid expands when frozen, so leave space in the container or bag so that the casserole has room to expand.

- Label the freezer bag with the name of the dish and the date frozen. One casserole looks much like another when frozen.

If you want to keep the frozen casseroles a long time, here are a few points to remember.
- Use rice flour for thickening. If you use ordinary flour or cornflour the sauce can separate after freezing.

- Be sparing with the onion, and herbs and spices. These flavours tend to become much stronger when frozen for any length of time.

CHICKEN LIVERS PAYSANNE

Serves: 4

1 onion, chopped
4 tablespoons butter or margarine
750 g (1½ lb) chicken livers, chopped
1 teaspoon marjoram
2 teaspoons chopped parsley
3 tablespoons red wine
1 cup sour cream
salt and pepper

Fry onion in butter or margarine. Add chicken livers and cook for 5 minutes. Add marjoram, parsley, wine, sour cream, salt and pepper to taste. Simmer for 5 minutes more and serve with hot boiled rice.

Note: Chicken Livers Paysanne may also be cooked in a lidded casserole dish in a moderately slow oven for 15-20 minutes or until tender.

LAMB KIDNEY STEW

Serves: 4

1 x 750 g (1½ lb) lamb's kidney
1 tablespoon plain flour
2 rashers bacon, finely chopped
1 tablespoon butter or margarine
½ cup sliced celery
1 large onion, chopped
1 cup tinned tomatoes or fresh chopped
   tomatoes
1 green pepper, chopped
1 teaspoon salt
freshly ground black pepper
½ cup beef stock (see page 154) or water

Wash kidney and parboil in salted water to cover for 15 minutes to remove odours. Remove from water, rinse well and drain. Cut kidney in half, remove fat and tubes, cut into 1 cm (½ inch) slices and coat them with flour. Chop bacon rashers finely and fry gently in a pan until lightly coloured. Add butter or margarine and brown kidney pieces with the bacon. Add celery and onions and cook, stirring, until onion is soft. Add tomatoes, green pepper, salt and pepper and stock. Stir well, cover and simmer for 30-45 minutes or until kidney is tender and serve hot with boiled rice or macaroni noodles, and carrots or a green vegetable.

Note: Lamb Kidney Stew can also be cooked in a lidded casserole dish in a moderately slow oven for ½-1 hour or until tender.

TRIPE RAGOÛT

Serves: 3-4

500 g (1 lb) tripe
1 whole onion
2 teaspoons salt
3 tablespoons butter or margarine
1 onion, chopped
1 clove garlic, crushed
1 cup skinned, chopped tomatoes
1 bay leaf, 3 parsley stalks, tied together
½ teaspoon thyme
½ teaspoon marjoram
½ teaspoon paprika

Wash tripe and blanch by placing in a saucepan of cold water, bringing it to the boil and pouring off the water. Cover tripe with fresh cold water, add whole onion and salt and bring to the boil, reduce heat and simmer gently for 1½-2 hours or until just tender. Remove tripe from liquid and cut into thin strips about 2.5 cm (1 inch) long. Reserve liquid.

In another saucepan, melt butter or margarine and fry chopped onion and garlic until soft. Add strips of tripe and cook for a few minutes, then add tomatoes, bay leaf and parsley stalks, herbs and paprika. Strain off ½ cup tripe liquid and add to saucepan. Cover and simmer for 30-45 minutes or until sauce is thickened. Remove flavouring bouquet and serve Tripe Ragoût hot with mashed potatoes and a green vegetable or glazed carrots.

Note: The second cooking may be done in a lidded casserole dish in a moderately slow oven for ¾ hour or until tender.

STUFFED HEARTS

Serves: 4

Stuffing
1 onion, chopped
2 tablespoons butter or margarine
1½ cups soft breadcrumbs
1 cup diced celery
1 tablespoon chopped parsley
½ teaspoon mixed herbs
salt and pepper

Hearts
4 sheep's hearts
2 tablespoons butter or margarine
1½ cups beef stock (see page 154) or water and beef stock cubes
1-2 tablespoons cornflour
salt and pepper

To prepare stuffing: Fry the onion in the butter or margarine until soft, but not brown. Combine with the remaining stuffing ingredients and mix thoroughly. Season to taste with salt and pepper.

To prepare hearts: Wash the hearts and trim off excess fat and any large blood vessels. To make one cavity for stuffing cut out the wall dividing the two cavities of the heart. Dry the cavities with a clean cloth. Fill the hearts with the stuffing and close the opening with small skewers laced together with fine string, or sew with coarse cotton. Melt the butter in a saucepan and fry the hearts until brown all over. Add the stock. Cover and simmer for 1½-2 hours or until tender. Mix the cornflour to a paste with a little cold water, stir into the saucepan and bring to the boil stirring continuously. Season to taste with salt and pepper. Remove the string or cotton from the hearts before serving. Serve hot with gravy poured over, or cold with salad.

Variation: Instead of beef stock try using water and a dry packet soup: mushroom, tomato, celery or vegetable are all excellent.

Note: Stuffed Hearts may also be cooked in a lidded casserole dish in a moderately slow oven for 1½-2 hours or until tender.

KIDNEYS IN WHITE WINE

Serves: 2-3

500 g (1 lb) kidneys, lamb, pork or ox
1 cup white wine, or ¼ cup port or Marsala
6 large onions, chopped
2 tablespoons oil
2 tablespoons butter or margarine
4 tablespoons chopped parsley

Pour boiling water over kidneys in a bowl and leave to stand for about 5 minutes, then remove skin and white core from kidneys and cut into thin slices. Marinate slices in white wine, port or Marsala for 1 hour. Fry the onions very slowly in oil and butter or margarine in a covered pan until softened, but not browned. Add kidneys and the wine marinade, then cover again and simmer gently for 20-30 minutes or until kidneys are tender. Remove lid and boil quickly until most of the wine has evaporated, leaving a thick sauce. Tip kidney slices and sauce into a serving dish and sprinkle with chopped parsley. Serve with fluffy mashed potatoes.

Variation: Red wine, sherry, cider or vermouth may be substituted for the white wine, port or Marsala. You can also add ½ cup sliced mushrooms for additional flavour at the same time as the kidneys.

Note: Kidneys in White Wine may also be cooked in a lidded casserole dish in a moderately slow oven for 15-30 minutes, or until tender.

CHICKEN LIVERS SUPREME

Serves: 4

½ cup olive oil
4 tablespoons butter or margarine
2 cups finely chopped onion
2 cloves garlic, crushed
250 g (8 oz) chicken livers, chopped
6 rashers bacon, finely chopped
½ cup finely chopped parsley
1 green pepper, finely chopped
1 kg (2 lb) tomatoes, peeled and chopped,
   or use equal quantity of canned tomatoes
⅓ cup red wine
salt and pepper
500 g (1 lb) spaghetti or vermicelli

Heat olive oil and butter or margarine in a frying pan. Add onion and garlic and fry till golden. Add chicken livers and gently fry till brown and stiffened. Add bacon, parsley and pepper. Cover and simmer for 10 minutes. Stir in tomatoes, wine, salt and pepper. Simmer, covered, for 20 minutes, stirring occasionally. Meanwhile, cook spaghetti until tender, drain and turn into a hot serving dish. Pour livers over spaghetti and serve.

Note: Chicken Livers Supreme can also be cooked in a lidded casserole dish in a moderately slow oven for 15-30 minutes or until tender.

LAMBS' TONGUES WITH RAISIN SAUCE

Serves: 4-6

Lambs' Tongues
6 lambs' tongues
1 onion
1 clove garlic
1 bay leaf
1 teaspoon salt

Raisin Sauce
1 cup stock from tongues
¼ cup raisins
¼ cup brown sugar
¼ cup dry white wine
1 tablespoon cornflour
salt
freshly ground black pepper

To prepare tongues: Rinse tongues, place in saucepan and cover with cold water. Add whole peeled onion, garlic, bay leaf and salt. Bring to a slow boil, cover, reduce heat and simmer gently for at least 2 hours, or until tongues are tender. Remove tongues, skin them and remove any bone and gristle from roots. Strain stock and reserve.

To prepare Raisin Sauce: Return 1 cup tongue stock to a clean saucepan, add raisins and brown sugar. Bring to the boil and stir in wine and cornflour mixed to a smooth paste. Add salt and pepper to taste. Reduce heat and stir constantly until sauce thickens. Add tongues and simmer for 20 minutes. Serve tongues, either whole or sliced lengthways, in the Raisin Sauce, with creamed, fried or duchesse potatoes and a green vegetable.

BAKED LIVER AND ONIONS

Serves: 4
Oven temperature: moderate

1 large onion
3 tablespoons butter or margarine
½ cup red wine
½ cup water
¼ cup chopped parsley
1 bay leaf, crumbled
1 teaspoon dried thyme
1 teaspoon salt
freshly ground black pepper
4 slices lamb's liver
plain flour to coat

Slice onion thickly, place in base of an ovenproof dish and dot with butter or margarine. Pour in wine and water and add parsley, bay leaf, thyme, salt and pepper. Cover and cook in a moderate oven for 30 minutes. Coat liver with flour and place on top of onion slices and herbs. Cover and bake for a further 30 minutes, basting with liquid occasionally. Remove cover and bake for a further 10 minutes. Serve hot with baked jacket potatoes and a green vegetable.

SPANISH CHICKEN LIVERS

Serves: 2-3
Oven temperature: moderately slow

500 g (1 lb) chicken livers
8 bacon rashers
1 cup mandarin segments or lychees,
   drained (approximately 1 medium can)
2 tablespoons butter or margarine
1 onion, chopped
1 clove garlic, crushed (optional)
2 tablespoons plain flour
½ cup port, Madeira or sherry
½ cup water
1 chicken stock cube
1 tablespoon tomato paste
salt and pepper

Trim gristle and membrane from chicken livers and leave whole. Remove bacon rinds and halve each rasher. Drain mandarin segments or lychees well and place one mandarin segment or one lychee on top of each chicken liver. Wrap halved bacon rashers around each liver, and secure with a toothpick. Fry wrapped livers in hot butter or margarine until browned. Remove from pan and place in a casserole dish. Add onion and garlic to the pan and fry until softened, then sprinkle with flour and fry till golden brown. Off the heat add port, Madeira or sherry, water, and crumbled stock cube. Stir well then return to heat and simmer for a few minutes. Add all other ingredients and stir well. Pour sauce over chicken livers in casserole, cover and cook in a moderately slow oven for 30-45 minutes or until tender and sauce is well thickened.

Variation: Fresh green grapes can be substituted for the mandarin segments or lychees.

Note: This recipe will serve 4-6 people as a first course.

SWEETBREADS WITH CREAM

Serves: 3-4
Oven temperature: moderately slow

500 g (1 lb) sweetbreads
salt and pepper
1 large carrot, chopped
1 large onion, chopped
2 cups chicken stock (see page 154) or
   water and chicken stock cubes
2 teaspoons arrowroot or cornflour
½ cup double cream

Wash sweetbreads well, blanch in boiling water, rinse in cold water and trim. Season and place in an ovenproof casserole dish on a bed of carrot and onion. Add stock and cover dish with buttered greaseproof paper and a lid. Cook in a moderately slow oven for 1 hour. Strain off the cooking liquor into a saucepan and thicken with arrowroot or cornflour blended to a smooth paste with a little cold water. Add cream and reheat without boiling. Serve sweetbreads coated with the sauce.

TRIPE AND ONIONS

Serves: 3-4

500 g (1 lb) tripe
2 white onions
2 teaspoons salt
2 tablespoons butter or margarine
3 tablespoons plain flour
1¼ cups cooking liquid from tripe
1¼ cups milk
1 tablespoon chopped parsley
pepper if desired

Wash tripe and scrape underside if necessary. Blanch by placing in a saucepan of cold water, bringing it to the boil and pouring off the water.

Cut blanched tripe into pieces about 2.5 cm (1 inch) square. Replace in a clean saucepan, cover with cold water, add whole peeled white onions and salt. Bring to the boil, reduce heat and simmer gently until tender, 1½-3 hours (the time depends on the degree of cooking already done by the butcher). Drain off liquid and reserve 1¼ cups. Place tripe on a plate and cut onions into pieces. In the same saucepan melt butter or margarine and stir in flour. Cook over a medium heat for 1-2 minutes then pour in tripe liquid and milk and bring to the boil, stirring continuously, until thick and bubbling. Stir in tripe, onions, parsley and pepper if desired. Serve hot with bacon rolls, toast triangles and a green vegetable.

Fishing for compliments

When you look at these seafood recipes you may ask what they are doing in a casserole recipe book. Well, if you define a casserole as I do — food cooked in liquid in a covered pot at a slow, low temperature — then all these recipes are casseroles.

Casseroling is one of the best ways to cook fish. Baking a whole fish with wine in a covered dish on a low, slow heat is the true casserole method. One controversial point is the timing: fish barely needs to be cooked at all. The most common mistake in fish cooking is overcooking, which results in dry, tough chunks instead of delicate, subtle, moist, melting mouthfuls. To achieve the latter results, keep the temperature low and the cooking time short.

Scallops need only a few minutes — 2 to 4 minutes at the most — in barely simmering liquid.

Cooked prawns need reheating only. Double cooking makes prawns tough as old boots — so don't bubble and boil cooked prawns for a long time in a mornay sauce.

Mussels need to be cooked only till their shells open. So either make the casserole sauce before adding the mussels, or (as I prefer) toss the mussels into a tomato, garlic sauce. Let them open and release their own superb liquor, and then quickly remove the mussels to stop them cooking longer and toughening. Then concoct the sauce by simmering, seasoning and possibly boiling and reducing down. Keep salt to a minimum though, for the mussel liquid is usually loaded with salty water.

Lobsters: the cooking time depends on the size. Large lobster will need longer cooking, but it is easy to tell if crustaceans are cooked because the colour will change from greyish brown to bright red. The times range from 15-20 minutes for large specimens down to only about 10 minutes for the small fry.

Fish: again this depends on the flesh of the fish, its size, and whether it's whole or cut into chunks. But it's easy really. When the flesh changes from floppy and translucent to firm and white the fish is cooked. A simple test is to push a knife through the flesh, pressing lightly down. When the flesh flakes into white all the way through, it's done — overcooking will dry fish out.

STOCKS

1 *Fish stock,* made with fish bones and heads, chopped vegetables, water and wine. See page 154.

2 *Chicken stock,* made with cooked or uncooked chicken bones, chopped vegetables, water and seasonings. See page 154.

3 *Easy stock.* For instant stock that's full of flavour substitute canned condensed beef consomme, undiluted for the stock called for in the recipe. This is great for really rich flavour in those extra special recipes.

4 *Stock from instant cubes.* To give stock cubes some extra flavour just boil together 4 stock cubes with 3 cups water, 1 cup white wine and ½ cup chopped onion, celery and carrot. Simmer 20 minutes then strain and use.

Top: Squid in Red Wine (page 91);
bottom: Mediterranean Prawns (page 93)

TUNA CASSEROLE

Serves: 2-3
Oven temperature: moderately hot

**1 packet of sherry sauce mix, made up
with milk according to instructions
on the packet or 1 cup white sauce
flavoured with 2 tablespoons dry
sherry**
**1 large tin chunky tuna (about 500 g or
16 oz)**
**250 g (8 oz) canned or fresh button
mushrooms**
**1 can whole peeled tomatoes (about 425 g
or 15 oz)**
1 teaspoon parsley flakes
**¼ cup grated Cheddar or assorted cheese
or 2 tablespoons grated Parmesan
cheese**
3 tablespoons dry breadcrumbs
sprinkling of paprika

Grease a casserole dish. Make up the sherry sauce and gently mix it with the tuna, mushrooms, tomatoes and parsley, taking care not to break up the tuna. Spoon this mixture into the casserole dish and top with a mixture of grated cheese and breadcrumbs. Sprinkle with paprika. Bake in a moderately hot oven for 15-20 minutes or until crisp and golden brown and well heated through. Serve with buttered noodles or macaroni.

SQUID IN RED WINE

Serves: 2-3
Oven temperature: moderately slow

500 g (1 lb) squid, well cleaned
4 tablespoons olive oil
2 onions, sliced
1-2 cloves garlic, crushed
1 cup red, white or rosé wine
bouquet garni (see page 82)
1 strip of lemon peel
salt and pepper
**1 can tomatoes, drained (about 425 g or
15 oz)**

Slice the squid into rounds, including the tentacles. Heat oil in a frying pan. Add onions and garlic and fry until well softened. Add squid rings and fry for 1-2 minutes. Add all other ingredients to pan and stir to combine. Transfer into a casserole dish. Cover and cook in a moderately slow oven for 1-1½ hours or until tender, or squid may be cooked on top of the stove over a very low heat. Serve with plainly cooked fluffy rice.

Note: This recipe will serve 4-6 people as a first course.

STUFFED FISH FILLETS

Serves: 3-4
Oven temperature: moderate

4 tablespoons fresh white breadcrumbs
pinch of tarragon
4 tablespoons sliced mushrooms
1 onion, thinly sliced
2 tablespoons chopped parsley
1 teaspoon grated lemon rind
1 egg
500 g (1 lb) fish fillets
½ cup dry white wine or cider vinegar

Mix the breadcrumbs, tarragon, mushrooms, onion, parsley and lemon rind with the egg. Spread mixture on top of half the fish fillets and then put remaining fillets on top to form a sort of sandwich. Secure with cocktail sticks. Place fillets in a baking dish and pour white wine over them. Bake in a moderate oven for 20 minutes.

Left: Pumpkin without Parallel (page 110);
right: Vegetable Casserole (page 111)

BREAM WITH WHITE WINE

Serves: 6
Oven temperature: moderate

1 x sea bream, about 1.5 kg (3 lb)
¾ cup thinly sliced mushrooms
1 onion, thinly sliced
salt and pepper
1 bay leaf
pinch of thyme
1 cup fresh breadcrumbs
4 tablespoons butter or margarine
1¾ cups dry white wine (hock)
2 limes or lemons

Clean fish and place in a flat buttered ovenproof dish. Cover with mushrooms and onion and season with salt and pepper. Add bay leaf and sprinkle with thyme and breadcrumbs. Dot fish with butter or margarine and cover with wine. Cover and bake in a moderate oven for 40 minutes or until fish is tender. Serve with wedges of lime or lemon.

LUXURY BAKED FISH

Serves: 6-8
Oven temperature: moderately slow

Stuffing
125 g (4 oz) scallops
125 g (4 oz) cooked prawns, peeled
2 tablespoons butter or margarine
6 oysters
1½ cups boiled or fried rice
grated rind 1 lemon
salt and pepper

Fish
1 x 2 kg (4 lb) (approximate weight)
   fish suitable for baking whole
   (halibut or sea bream)
½ cup white wine or water
2 tablespoons oil

To prepare stuffing: Gently fry scallops in butter or margarine for 1-2 minutes to partially cook. Drain oysters and mix with scallops, prawns, lemon rind and rice, mix well and season to taste.

To prepare fish: Get fish shop to scale and gut fish. Spoon stuffing into fish cavity and secure with a long metal skewer. Place in a baking dish or oven bag, add the white wine or water and oil, cover with a lid or tie oven bag and pierce with a fork. Bake in a moderately slow oven until flesh flakes easily, about 1 hour.

MARINATED HALIBUT

Serves: 2
Oven temperature: slow

500 g (1 lb) halibut steaks
1 onion, thinly sliced
½ lemon, thinly sliced
1 clove garlic, crushed
salt and pepper
1 tablespoon olive oil
¾ cup dry white wine
aluminium foil
2 tablespoons double cream

Place fish steaks in an ovenproof dish. Arrange onion and lemon on top. Sprinkle with garlic, salt and pepper and pour over olive oil and wine. Cover with aluminium foil. Place in refrigerator and allow to marinate overnight.

Cook in a slow oven for 15 minutes. Stir cream into sauce before serving.

Note: This recipe is also suitable for any oily fleshed fish, such as mullet, mackerel, pilchards or fresh tuna.

BAKED CIDER TROUT

Serves: 5-6
Oven temperature: moderate

5-6 medium-sized trout
juice of 1 lemon
1 teaspoon salt
1 clove garlic
1 cup cider
1 orange, sliced
2 tablespoons each chopped parsley,
    spring onion and dry breadcrumbs
4 tablespoons melted butter or
    margarine

Wash trout and dry with paper towels, rub skin with lemon juice and sprinkle with salt. Sprinkle the crushed garlic in the base of a well buttered shallow casserole, large enough to hold trout in a single layer. Place trout in dish, arrange orange slices on top, and pour cider over them. Sprinkle with parsley, spring onion and dry breadcrumbs, then spoon butter or margarine evenly over all. Cover and bake in a moderate oven for 20-30 minutes. Serve with fluffy mashed potatoes.

MEDITERRANEAN PRAWNS

Serves: 4-6

Stock
1 kg (2 lb) approximate weight, fish
    scraps, skin, heads and bones
prawn peelings and heads
3-4 cups dry white wine
large strip lemon peel

Prawns
2 onions, chopped
1 red pepper, cored and sliced
1 green pepper, cored and sliced
2 tablespoons olive oil
2-4 cloves garlic, crushed
500 g (1 lb) peeled tomatoes or use
    canned tomatoes
750 g-1 kg (1½-2 lb) cooked prawns,
    peeled

To prepare stock: Ask the fish man to give you fish heads and scraps for the stock. Put them with prawn peelings, white wine and torn up lemon peel into a saucepan, bring to the boil and simmer 15-20 minutes. Liquidise in a blender or mash up well with a wooden spoon. Strain well.

To prepare prawns: Fry onion and peppers in oil till softened. Add all other ingredients, including stock, except prawns. Cover with a lid and simmer gently for about ¾ hour or until thickened and flavours are well combined. Add prawns, stirring well to coat with the sauce.

This is an excellent recipe to prepare in advance. Make the sauce and add the prawns, then leave till needed, reheating just before serving. Serve with buttered macaroni or fried rice.

CURRIED SCALLOPS

Serves: 4-6

1 tablespoon oil, butter or margarine
2 medium-sized onions, chopped
2 cloves garlic, crushed
1 tablespoon curry paste
2 cups coconut milk (see page 157)
salt to taste
1 tablespoon tomato puree
500 g (1 lb) scallops
chopped parsley and lemon wedges for
    garnish

Heat oil, butter or margarine in a saucepan and fry onion until it starts to soften. Stirring continuously, add garlic and curry paste, and continue cooking until ingredients are golden brown. Add coconut milk and mix thoroughly. Season to taste with salt and add tomato purée. Cook sauce over a moderate heat until it thickens.

Add scallops to sauce, cook for 5-7 minutes, depending on size, until cooked. Serve immediately on a bed of boiled rice and garnish with chopped parsley and lemon wedges.

CLASSIC SCALLOPS

Serves: 2

large strip lemon peel (optional)
1 cup dry white wine
6 spring onions, chopped
500 g (1 lb) scallops
5 tablespoons butter or margarine
2 tablespoons plain flour
½ cup double cream
salt and pepper
125 g (4 oz) mushrooms, sliced
½ cup water chestnuts, sliced
    (optional)
2 tablespoons dry breadcrumbs
3 tablespoons grated cheese

Tear the lemon leaves into a few pieces. Put wine, shallots and lemon leaves in a saucepan and simmer 5 minutes. Add scallops and bring back to the boil then top with a lid and remove the pot from the stove and stand for 5 minutes. With this method the scallops cook, but stay meltingly tender. When cooked, drain, reserving liquid. Melt 3 tablespoons of the butter or margarine in a pan. Add flour and cook for 1-2 minutes. Off the heat add scallop liquid, stir well and bring back to the boil, simmer for a few minutes. Add cream and salt and pepper to taste. Fry mushrooms in remaining butter or margarine till tender. Add to the sauce with scallops and sliced water chestnuts. Stir, then tip into a flameproof serving dish. Sprinkle with a mixture of breadcrumbs and cheese. This can be prepared in advance to this point and then kept until serving time. Reheat under the grill, or in a moderate oven, until brown and cheese has melted.

Note: With most seafood recipes it is best to use a quality wine in the cooking. I generally use the same wine I am going to drink with the dish. As a rule, the better the wine, the better the sauce. This recipe will serve 4 as a first course.

POACHED FISH IN WHITE WINE SAUCE

Serves: 4-6

1½ cups dry white wine
pinch of tarragon
1 small onion, finely chopped
1 kg (2 lb) fish fillets
3 egg yolks
3 tablespoons double cream
salt and pepper

Mix wine, tarragon and chopped onion in a large saucepan. Add fish, heat gently till simmering and poach till tender. Drain fish well and keep hot. Boil cooking liquid continuously until reduced to half. Beat egg yolks with cream, add to cooled liquid and reheat gently, without boiling. Add salt and pepper to taste, pour over the poached fish fillets, and serve hot.

CREAMED HADDOCK

Serves: 6-8
Oven temperature: moderately slow

1 kg (2 lb) smoked haddock or cod fillets
2 tablespoons butter or margarine
2 tablespoons plain flour
1½ cups milk
1½ cups double cream
salt and pepper
125 g (4 oz) mushrooms, sliced and
   cooked in butter
¼ teaspoon Tabasco sauce
1 small onion, grated
1 teaspoon Worcestershire sauce
pinch dry mustard
2 tablespoons dry sherry

Soak haddock or cod fillets in cold water for several hours, drain, and remove bones and skin. Break into pieces. Melt butter or margarine in a saucepan, blend in flour until smooth, cook for 2-3 minutes. Gradually add milk and cream, stirring continuously until sauce is thick and smooth. Season to taste with salt and pepper. Add mushrooms, Tabasco sauce, onion, Worcestershire sauce, mustard and dry sherry and blend together. Pour a layer of cream sauce into the base of an ovenproof casserole, add a layer of fish. Season to taste with extra salt and pepper. Repeat layers until all ingredients are used, finishing with a layer of sauce. Place casserole in a baking dish containing approximately 2 cm (¾ inch) depth of water. Cook in a moderately slow oven for approximately 1 hour. Serve piping hot with toast or boiled rice.

BAKED HALIBUT
WITH HAZELNUTS AND PRAWNS

Serves: 6-8
Oven temperature: slow

1 halibut, about 2 kg (4 lb)
1 cup dry white wine
1 tablespoon chopped fresh fennel or dill
   (or ½ teaspoon dry powdered fennel or
   dill)
2 medium onions
1 medium carrot
1 clove garlic, crushed
salt and pepper
2 tablespoons butter or margarine
½ cup hazelnuts or almonds
extra fennel or dill
½ kg (1 lb) cooked prawns, peeled
2-3 teaspoons cornflour
1 cup double cream

Clean and scale fish, or have your fishmonger do it for you, and place in a greased ovenproof serving dish or baking dish. Place wine, fennel or dill, one chopped onion, chopped carrot, garlic and seasoning into a saucepan and simmer with a lid on for 15-20 minutes. Pour this stock over the prepared fish, cover, and bake in a slow oven until the flesh is white and flakes easily, about 30-45 minutes.

While the fish is cooking prepare the sauce. Chop the other onion and fry in the saucepan with the butter or margarine, nuts, and a bit of extra fennel or dill until the nuts are golden brown. Add prawns and heat through. Move to one side until fish has finished cooking.

Carefully pour off the liquid from the fish, holding fish in place with an egg slice. Add 1 cup of liquid to the nuts and prawn mixture and bring to the boil. Blend cornflour with a little cold water to make a smooth cream and add a little hot liquid to it then pour cornflour mixture into the sauce. Bring to the boil and simmer 2 minutes to thicken. Remove from heat, add cream, stir and pour over the fish. Serve with boiled or fried rice.

CELERY FISH FILLETS

Serves: 4
Oven temperature: moderately hot

4 fresh fish fillets
1 can cream of celery soup (about 440g
    or 15 oz)
½ cup grated cheese
2 tablespoons cornflakes

Arrange fish in a layer in a buttered, shallow baking dish. Stir celery soup in can and pour over fish. Top with cheese and cornflakes mixed together. Bake in a moderately hot oven for 20 minutes or until tender.

GREEK SHRIMP WITH FETA CHEESE

Serves: 4-6
Oven temperature: moderate

⅓ cup Greek olive oil
1 large white onion, chopped
1 can Italian peeled and seeded plum
    tomatoes, about 500 g (16 oz)
4 cloves garlic, finely chopped
125 g (4 oz) jar or tin sweet red pimento
    or red peppers
3 tablespoons tomato paste
½ cup red wine
Tabasco or chilli sauce
salt and freshly ground pepper
1 kg (2 lb) large Dublin Bay green prawns
3-4 tablespoons butter or margarine
1 lemon
250 g (8 oz) feta cheese
small bunch parsley

Heat olive oil in a medium-sized saucepan, add onion and fry till golden. Add tomatoes, garlic and chopped, drained sweet red peppers or pimento. Stir in tomato paste, wine and one or two drops Tabasco or chilli sauce. Season with salt and pepper to taste. Mix together thoroughly and simmer, uncovered, for 30 minutes, till thick but not dry. If sauce gets too thick add more wine; if too thin boil briskly for 2 or 3 minutes to thicken. Wash, shell and devein the prawns. Put prawns into a shallow ovenproof dish. Squeeze juice of half the lemon into sauce, stir and pour over prawns. Top with feta cheese cut into chunks and bake, uncovered, in a moderate oven until cheese is soft, about 15-20 minutes.

Just before serving squeeze other half of lemon over dish, add a little more ground pepper and sprinkle with chopped parsley. Serve at once before cheese has time to set.

GREEN PRAWNS WITH ROSEMARY

Serves: 6

3 tablespoons olive oil
1.5 kg (3 lb) fresh green Dublin Bay
    prawns, unpeeled
6 cloves garlic, finely chopped
6-8 stalks fresh rosemary
1 teaspoon salt
½ teaspoon freshly ground black pepper
½ cup dry white wine
1 tablespoon chopped parsley

Heat oil in a frying pan, add prawns and garlic and toss for a few seconds. Strip rosemary leaves from stalks and add to pan with salt, pepper, wine and parsley. Simmer for 10 minutes. Transfer prawns to a heated serving dish and pour the remaining juice over them. Serve with a white wine.

ITALIAN MARINARA

Serves: 6-8

1 kg (2 lb) cooked shellfish (oysters,
**   scallops, prawns and/or lobster)**
¼ cup olive oil
1 onion, finely chopped
2 cloves garlic, sliced
1 kg (2 lb) tomatoes, peeled and chopped,
**   or use chopped canned tomatoes**
1½ teaspoons salt
1 teaspoon oregano
1 teaspoon chopped parsley
¼ teaspoon pepper
¼ cup red or white wine (optional)
375 g (12 oz) spaghetti

Shell the fish, wash and drain. Fry gently in medium hot oil till softened and almost cooked. Remove from pan. Add onion and garlic and fry till golden. Stir in tomatoes, salt, oregano, parsley, pepper and wine. Cover and cook rapidly for 15 minutes or until thickened, stirring occasionally. Add shellfish and reheat gently. While tomato mixture is cooking, cook the spaghetti in plenty of boiling water. Drain. Serve immediately with shellfish sauce poured over it.

SEAFOOD BAKE

Serves: 2-3
Oven temperature: moderate

250 g (8 oz) crabmeat
¼ cup melted butter or margarine
2 tablespoons plain flour
2 teaspoons salt
1 teaspoon paprika
½ teaspoon ground white pepper
1 onion, finely chopped
3 cups milk
½ cup dry sherry
3 eggs, separated
20-24 oysters, drained
125 g (4 oz) shaped pasta, cooked
¼ cup buttered breadcrumbs
2 tablespoons capers

Reserve a few pieces of crabmeat for garnish and cut the remainder into chunks. Melt the butter, stir in the flour with the salt, paprika, pepper and onion. Add the milk, stir well, then cook over a low heat until thickened, stirring all the time. Add the dry sherry, beaten egg yolks, crabmeat and oysters to the sauce. Cool a little then mix in the drained pasta and stiffly beaten egg whites. Spoon into a greased casserole dish. Cook in a moderate oven for 35-40 minutes. Top with reserved crabmeat and sprinkle with the buttered breadcrumbs and drained capers. Put back in the oven for 10-15 minutes until top is crisp and brown.

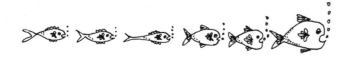

POACHED FISH IN WINE

Serves: 4
Oven temperature: moderate

4 small whole fish or 4 fish fillets (see method)
2 tablespoons butter or margarine
1 onion, thinly sliced
2½ cups white wine
salt and pepper
lemon slices and parsley sprigs for garnish

Place prepared fish in a greased ovenproof dish. Add butter and margarine, onion, wine, salt and pepper and cover tightly with greased aluminium foil. Place in a moderate oven for 15 minutes or till tender. Drain and serve immediately, garnished with slices of lemon and parsley sprigs.

Note: This recipe is suitable for whole deep sea or river fish less than 500 g (1 lb) in weight or for fish fillets.

LOBSTER A LA MICHEL

Serves: 2-4

1 x 1 kg (2 lb) lobster
¼ cup olive oil
2 tomatoes, chopped
1 onion, thinly sliced
½ teaspoon crushed garlic
1½ cups dry white wine
¾ cup cream
1 teaspoon paprika

Prepare lobster for cooking and cut meat into slices 1 cm (½ inch) thick. Heat olive oil in a large frying pan and fry lobster over a high heat for 1 minute on both sides. Add tomatoes, onion, garlic, wine, cream and paprika. Top with a lid and cook for a further 15 minutes. Serve hot with saffron rice.

Up the garden path

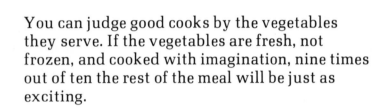

You can judge good cooks by the vegetables they serve. If the vegetables are fresh, not frozen, and cooked with imagination, nine times out of ten the rest of the meal will be just as exciting.

It's very easy to be lazy when cooking vegetables and to just prepare carrots, potatoes and frozen peas by popping them into boiling water and serving with a dab of butter stuck on top. However, you can just as easily give vegetables a new lease of life and prepare a dish worthy of standing alone as a separate course — the French have been doing it for years. You can also serve vegetables as a first course.

It doesn't take much more time to prepare vegetables interestingly and it will be a welcome change. For example, try Scalloped Potatoes. It's just slices of potato cooked in cream with a squash of garlic and a grate of cheese on top. Simple? Yes, but so delicious with its crusty topping. Cooked in one big pot it's a marvellous side dish for the main course. Try slicing the spuds into individual ramekins — this makes a stunning 'starter'. Or try ratatouille. It's just a casserole of mixed vegetables, prepared in the French way. A very versatile concoction, it can be served hot or cold, anytime during the meal. Ratatouille also makes a scrumptious sauce to pour over meat, or a delicious side vegetable dish, or an exciting salad. I always make ratatouille in triplicate.

CHOPPING VEGETABLES

1 *Peppers.* Remove centre core and seeds, and then wash well to remove any remaining seeds. Slice into thin rounds. I use a small serrated knife for chopping vegetables with a smooth skin like pepper or tomato. A serrated knife is most efficient if used with a sawing action.

Celery. For dicing or chopping celery, slice each stalk vertically, but leave one end uncut so strips are attached. Now chop across the strips to give small, even-sized pieces.

Carrots. Cut into thin rounds or chop into chunks with a large chef's knife.

2
3 *To use the knife for chopping herbs.* Hold knife point with one hand and lift the handle of the knife with the other hand, then chop with an up and down motion. Sweep the herbs together with the knife every so often.

My most important chopping knife is a large chef's knife with a long straight blade. The blade is deep enough to allow my hand to grip the handle firmly without my knuckles being squashed when the blade is flat (see 3). The knife feels very heavy, but it is well balanced and the weight helps in the chopping because the blade tends to fall through the food with less effort on my part.

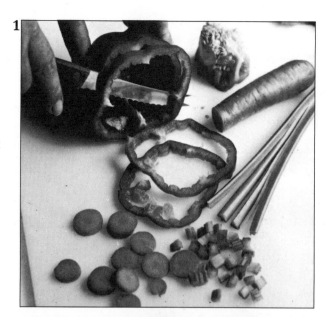

SPINACH CASSEROLE

Serves: 4
Oven temperature: moderate

2 bunches fresh spinach
1½ teaspoons salt
pinch pepper
2 tablespoons melted butter or
**   margarine**
2 eggs, lightly beaten
1 cup milk
1½ cups grated Swiss cheese
1 onion, finely chopped
breadcrumbs
extra grated Swiss cheese

Wash spinach and put wet leaves into a saucepan. Cook lightly, for about 3 minutes, with no extra liquid. Drain and chop finely. Mix spinach, salt, pepper, butter or margarine, eggs, milk, cheese and onions, then pour into a shallow baking dish or casserole. Lightly sprinkle breadcrumbs and extra cheese on top. Cover and bake in a moderate oven 45 minutes or till set. Remove lid 10 minutes before end of cooking to allow top to brown.

CASSEROLE VEGETABLE PIE

Serves: 6
Oven temperature: moderate

Vegetables
1 cauliflower
1 green or red pepper
4 eggs, hard-boiled
2 carrots
60 g (2 oz) shelled almonds
60 g (2 oz) butter or margarine
12 shallots
1 tablespoon chopped parsley

Topping
4 tablespoons butter or margarine
2 tablespoons plain flour
1 cup milk
1-2 teaspoons caraway seed
salt and pepper
1 cup breadcrumbs
½ cup grated cheese
2 teaspoons paprika

Wash cauliflower, break into flowerets and boil in salted water for 5 minutes, drain. Cut pepper into strips, discarding seeds. Shell and quarter eggs. Wash carrots and grate coarsely. Brown almonds in butter or margarine. Wash shallots and chop finely. Mix all ingredients together, including parsley, in a greased ovenproof dish.

To prepare topping: Melt butter or margarine in saucepan, stir in flour and add milk, stirring until thickened. Add caraway seed, salt and pepper. Pour over vegetables and top with breadcrumbs, cheese, and paprika. Cook in a moderate oven for 20-30 minutes until heated through and cheese is melted.

BAKED STUFFED AUBERGINE

Serves: 4
Oven temperature: moderate

1 aubergine
1 small onion, finely chopped
4 tablespoons butter or margarine
1 cup chopped ham
1 egg
¼ cup grated cheese
½ cup crumbled potato chips

Parboil whole, unpeeled aubergine for 10 minutes. Cut in half lengthways. Scoop out pulp from each half, leaving a 2.5 cm (1 inch) wall. Cut pulp into small pieces. Fry onion in butter or margarine till softened. Combine with aubergine pulp, ham and beaten egg. Spoon mixture into the hollowed halves, top with cheese and potato chips. Bake in a moderate oven for 25 minutes.

DUTCH RED CABBAGE

Serves: 3-4
Oven temperature: moderately slow

1 small red cabbage
2 tablespoons butter or margarine
1 onion, chopped
2 cooking apples, peeled and sliced
3 tablespoons white vinegar
3 tablespoons water
1 tablespoon sugar
salt and pepper
3 cloves

Shred the cabbage finely, removing hard stalks. Wash well then pour boiling water over the cabbage to blanch it. Drain. Melt butter or margarine in a saucepan and fry onion and apple over a low heat until soft. Mix together the vinegar, water and sugar. Remove onion and apple from the pan. Arrange alternating layers of cabbage and onion mixture in an ovenproof dish, sprinkling between each layer the vinegar mixture and salt and pepper. Add cloves then cover the dish with a tight lid and bake in a moderately slow oven for 1¼-1½ hours, or until cooked.

CARDAMOM AND SWEET POTATOES

Serves: 4
Oven temperature: moderate

500 g (1 lb) sweet potatoes
juice and grated rind of 1 orange
1 tablespoon honey
1 white onion, thinly sliced
salt
2 teaspoons ground cardamom seed
4 tablespoons butter or margarine
2 tablespoons breadcrumbs

Wash and peel potatoes and slice thinly. Mix orange juice, grated rind and honey together. Arrange potato slices and onion rings in a greased ovenproof dish, pour over the orange and honey mixture and sprinkle with salt and cardamom. Dot with butter or margarine and sprinkle with breadcrumbs. Bake in a moderate oven for 45 minutes. Serve hot.

GREEN AND WHITE CASSEROLE

Serves: 4

500 g (1 lb) green beans
1 small head cauliflower, or ½ a large
  one
4 tablespoons plain flour
5 tablespoons butter or margarine
1 cup milk
1 cup double cream
herb salt to season
pepper
butter or margarine for greasing dish
¼-½ cup toasted sliced almonds

String the beans and slice in half lengthwise then halve if beans are very long. Cook in boiling salted water until just tender, but still crunchy, 5-7 minutes. Break cauliflower into flowerets and cook in boiling salted water until only just done, about 6-8 minutes. Make a white sauce by cooking the flour and butter or margarine together in a small pan. Off the heat add milk and stir to combine. Return to heat, bring to boil and simmer a few minutes. It will be very thick at this stage. Remove from heat and stir in cream and seasonings. Heat again, but do not boil. Drain both vegetables well. Grease a casserole with butter or margarine. Add well drained vegetables and pour sauce over them. Sprinkle top with toasted almonds and serve. The dish may be made in advance and allowed to cool. When ready to serve heat through in a moderate oven for 10 minutes.

BRAISED LETTUCE

Serves: 4
Oven temperature: moderate

2 large lettuces
4 tablespoons butter or margarine
1 onion, thinly sliced
1 small carrot, thinly sliced
salt and pepper
3-4 rashers bacon, chopped
1 cup chicken stock (see page 154) or
water and chicken stock cube
1 teaspoon tomato paste
chopped parsley for garnish

Remove outside leaves and wash lettuces in cold water. Have ready a pan of boiling salted water. Cut each lettuce into quarters, drop into boiling water and boil for 3 minutes. Remove and plunge into cold water, drain and dry gently with a clean teatowel.

Pour melted butter or margarine into a casserole and add onion and carrot, then sprinkle with salt and pepper. Arrange the lettuce quarters on top, season with more salt and pepper and cover with bacon. Mix stock with tomato paste and pour over the lettuce, cover with buttered paper and braise for 40 minutes in a moderate oven. If necessary, add extra stock. Serve hot, sprinkled with chopped parsley.

AUBERGINE CASSEROLE

Serves: 4
Oven temperature: moderate

3 aubergines
salt
2 tablespoons oil
2 tablespoons tomato paste
1 cup yoghurt
pepper

Slice the aubergines, without peeling, into rounds and sprinkle with salt. Leave ½ an hour, then dry the slices and fry quickly in a frying pan in oil until coloured. Place slices into a round cake tin or ovenproof casserole as they come from the frying pan, layering them with tomato paste and yoghurt. Season with pepper. Cover the tin or casserole and bake in a moderate oven for 35-40 minutes. Turn out onto a serving plate and serve hot or cold.

EASY BRAISED CELERY

Serves: 4

1 head celery
3 tablespoons butter or margarine
2 tablespoons plain flour
1 cup chicken stock (see page 154) or
water and chicken stock cube
salt and pepper

Wash celery well, remove leaves and divide into neat pieces about 8 cm (3 inches) in length. Heat 2 tablespoons butter or margarine in a saucepan, toss the celery in this for 5-10 minutes until slightly brown on the outside. Remove celery and keep warm. Melt remaining butter or margarine in the pan and remove from heat to add flour, then cook for few minutes. Off heat, add liquid and stir well, then bring to boil, stirring continuously for about 5 minutes until thick. Add salt and pepper to taste. Return the celery to the pan and cook in the sauce over a very low heat, with the lid on, for approximately 1 hour.

Note: Easy Braised Celery may also be cooked in a lidded casserole dish in a moderately slow oven for ½-1 hour or until tender.

CABBAGE ROLLS

Serves: 3-4

8 big cabbage leaves
500 g (1 lb) minced steak or raw minced lamb
1 chopped onion
½ cup raw rice
salt and pepper
1 clove garlic, crushed
2 chicken stock cubes, crumbled
1-2 tablespoons chopped mint
lemon juice

Pack cabbage leaves into a basin, cover with boiling water and leave to one side for 5 minutes to soften. Drain, reserving the water. Cool a little. Mix together all other ingredients except lemon juice, mint and stock cubes. Place a few spoonfuls of meat mixture in each cabbage leaf. Fold over sides of leaf then roll up like a small parcel. Secure with toothpicks. Pack into a saucepan with joins downwards so parcels stay rolled up. Top with reserved cabbage water and stock cubes. Add mint and salt to taste. Cover with a lid and gently simmer 1-1½ hours. Remove rolls from liquid to a serving dish. Sprinkle with lemon juice. Serve hot or cold.

Variation: Use 1 can of tomatoes (about 425 g or 15 oz) instead of cabbage water for a more flavourful sauce.

Note: Cabbage Rolls can also be cooked in a lidded casserole dish in a moderately slow oven for 1-1½ hours or until tender.

SPICED RED CABBAGE

Serves: 3-4

2 tablespoons butter or margarine
1 onion, chopped
3 rashers bacon, rind removed and chopped
1 small red cabbage, washed and shredded
1 cooking apple
¼ cup raisins
1 x 430 g (14 oz) can beef broth with vegetables soup
¼ cup tomato ketchup
2 cups chopped leftover meat
1 tablespoon vinegar
pinch ground cloves
pinch caraway seeds
salt and pepper

Melt butter or margarine in frying pan and fry onion and bacon until softened. Add shredded red cabbage, the shredded apple, and raisins. Pour in beef broth and tomato ketchup. Cook until tender, about 45-60 minutes. Add chopped meat, vinegar, cloves and caraway seeds. Season to taste.

Note: Spiced Red Cabbage can also be cooked in a lidded casserole dish in a moderately slow oven for ¾-1 hour or until tender.

HUNGARIAN EGG AND CAULIFLOWER

Serves: 4-6
Oven temperature: moderate

4 potatoes, cooked and cut into slices
4 sliced hard-boiled eggs
125 g (4 oz) ham, diced or cut into strips
1 cauliflower, boiled until just tender in
**   salted water then divided into**
**   flowerets**
1 x 300 g (10 oz) carton sour cream
1 cup dry breadcrumbs
1 tablespoon butter or margarine

Grease a casserole dish. Arrange layers of potato slices, hard-boiled egg slices, ham, cauliflower flowerets and a layer of cream. Repeat these layers until all ingredients are used, finishing with sliced potatoes. Sprinkle with breadcrumbs and drizzle with melted butter or margarine. Cook in a moderate oven for 20-25 minutes or until top is golden brown.

CAULIFLOWER BAKE

Serves: 4-6
Oven temperature: moderate

Vegetable
1 medium-sized cauliflower
500 g (1 lb) spam, cubed
crushed potato chips

Cheese Sauce
2 tablespoons plain flour
2 tablespoons butter or margarine
1 cup milk
½ cup grated cheese

Break cauliflower into flowerets and cook until tender. Drain and arrange in an ovenproof dish. Top with devon sausage.

To prepare cheese sauce: Mix together the flour and butter or margarine in a small saucepan over gentle heat. Off the heat add the milk, stirring well. Replace on the heat and bring to the boil. Simmer a few minutes, add cheese and stir till melted.

Pour sauce over spam and cauliflower. Top with crushed potato crisps and bake in a moderate oven until hot and golden brown, about 30 minutes.

CREAMED CORN HAM 'N' EGGS

Serves: 4-5
Oven temperature: moderate

¾ cup butter or margarine
1 large white onion, finely chopped
500 g (1 lb) can sweet corn, cream style
250 g (8 oz) cooked ham or cooked bacon
3-4 eggs, hard-boiled
3 slices bread
1 tablespoon oil

Melt 3 tablespoons of the butter or margarine, fry onion until cooked but not browned and add sweet corn. Cut ham or bacon into small pieces, slice eggs and add to sweet corn and onion. Lightly fold together so that eggs are not broken too much. Put mixture into buttered ovenproof individual serving dishes, or one large dish. Cover with lid or aluminium foil and cook in a moderate oven for 20 minutes. Prepare croûtons from bread by dicing slices and frying in oil and remaining butter or margarine, drain well. Sprinkle croûtons over Creamed Corn, Ham 'n' Eggs before serving.

SCALLOPED CORN AND CARROTS

Serves: 4-6
Oven temperature: moderately hot

4½ tablespoons butter or margarine
1 cup chopped onion
2 teaspoons plain flour
½-1 teaspoon curry powder
1 teaspoon salt
1 teaspoon sugar
1 cup milk or milk and liquid from corn
1 cup corn, fresh cooked or tinned
1 cup diced and cooked carrots
1 cup stale bread diced in 5 mm (¼ inch) cubes

Melt 3 tablespoons of the butter or margarine in a saucepan, add chopped onion, stir, cover, and cook gently for 5 minutes until tender, but not browned. Add flour, curry powder, salt and sugar. Add the liquid in three portions, boiling and stirring well between additions. Fold the corn and carrots into the cooked sauce and pour mixture into an ovenproof dish. Melt the remaining butter or margarine, remove from heat and toss bread cubes in it. Sprinkle the buttered bread cubes over the vegetables. Bake, uncovered, in a moderately hot oven for 30-45 minutes. Serve with grilled meat and a green vegetable or salad.

Note: This dish may be prepared in advance, and reheated when needed.

SCALLOPED POTATOES

Serves: 6
Oven temperature: moderately hot

1 kg (2 lb) potatoes
3 tablespoons butter or margarine
1 clove garlic, crushed
salt and ground pepper
¾ cup grated cheese (Swiss or Cheddar)
1 cup milk

Peel potatoes and slice thinly. Rub a baking dish with ½ teaspoon of the butter or margarine. Soften the rest of the butter or margarine and mix with the crushed garlic, salt and pepper. Arrange the potato slices in layers in the baking dish, dotting with the garlic butter and a scattering of grated cheese between each layer.

Bring the milk to a boil and pour it over the potatoes. Top with a final layer of grated cheese and then bake in a moderately hot oven for 30-40 minutes or until the potatoes are tender when tested with a skewer.

CASSEROLE ALLA DRAGOMIROFF

Serves: 3-4
Oven temperature: moderately hot

500 g (1 lb) potatoes
500 g (1 lb) onions, chopped
4 tablespoons butter or margarine
500 g (1 lb) mushrooms, sliced
2-3 dill cucumbers
250 g (8 oz) Vienna frankfurters
1 cup undiluted condensed cream of mushroom or celery soup
1 cup grated cheese

Peel potatoes and boil until tender, drain and slice thickly. Fry onions in 2 tablespoons of the butter or margarine until tender then add mushrooms and cook till softened. Cut dill cucumbers and frankfurters into 1 cm (½ inch) pieces. Rub an ovenproof casserole with the rest of the butter or margarine. Arrange alternate layers of potato, frankfurters, onion, dill cucumber and mushrooms and then pour the undiluted soup over the top and sprinkle with grated cheese. Cook in a hot oven for approximately 30 minutes.

Preparation for Braised Beef Maman (page 123)

STUFFED GREEN PEPPERS

Serves: 4
Oven temperature: moderate

4 green peppers
1 tablespoon oil
4 tablespoons butter or margarine
salt and freshly ground black pepper
125 g (4 oz) rice
3 cups chicken stock (see page 154) or
water and chicken stock cubes
½ onion, finely chopped
60 g (2 oz) mushrooms, chopped
2 tablespoons oil
125 g (4 oz) cooked ham, finely chopped
2 tablespoons tomato paste
chopped parsley for garnish

Remove the tops of the peppers and reserve. Remove pith and seeds. Drop peppers in boiling water, add 1 tablespoon oil and boil for 5 minutes, drain well and dry. Place a small piece of butter or margarine in each pepper (using 2 tablespoons of the butter or margarine) and season well. Melt remaining butter or margarine in a frying pan. Add the rice and fry until golden. Cover with 1½ cups chicken stock and cook, stirring constantly, until the mixture comes to the boil. Reduce the heat, cover the pan, and cook slowly for 30 minutes, adding a little more chicken stock if necessary. Fry the onion and mushrooms in oil till softened and add to rice mixture. Mix in the ham, season well and spoon into peppers. Replace pepper tops and place stuffed peppers in a flat ovenproof dish. Blend tomato paste with remaining stock, pour over the stuffed peppers and bake in a moderate oven for 30-40 minutes or until cooked, basting frequently. Sprinkle with chopped parsley to serve.

RICOTTA STUFFED CANELLONI WITH TOMATO SAUCE

Serves: 4-6
Oven temperature: moderate

12 cannelloni
3 cups Ricotta cheese
½ cup chopped parsley
2 eggs
¾ cup Parmesan cheese
salt and pepper
dash of ground nutmeg
4-6 large ripe tomatoes, peeled and
chopped, or use equal quantity of
canned tomatoes
3 tablespoons olive oil
4 tablespoons (60 g or 2 oz) butter or
margarine

Cook cannelloni in boiling salted water according to directions on packet, or until just tender. When still a little firm, add 1-2 cups cold water and set aside till ready to fill.

Mix Ricotta cheese, parsley, eggs and ¼ cup of the Parmesan cheese thoroughly. Season to taste with salt, pepper and nutmeg. Place prepared tomatoes in a saucepan and cook, uncovered, until they become a thick pulp, stirring occasionally. Remove from heat and stir in oil gradually.

Drain cannelloni and fill with Ricotta cheese mixture. Place side by side in a single layer in a buttered shallow baking dish. Pour cooked tomato sauce around the cannelloni, sprinkle with remaining Parmesan cheese and dot with butter or margarine. Bake in a moderate oven about 20 minutes until bubbling. Serve at once.

Assorted ingredients for instant casseroles (pages 113-118)

PUMPKIN WITHOUT PARALLEL

Serves: 6-8
Oven temperature: moderately slow

1 medium-sized pumpkin
2 turnips
3 carrots
3 onions, sliced
3 sticks celery
2-4 cloves garlic, crushed
2 teaspoons salt
freshly ground pepper
280 ml (10 fluid oz) carton double cream
pinch nutmeg
1 chicken stock cube, crumbled
4 tablespoons butter or margarine

Slice off top of pumpkin or marrow. Remove seeds then scoop out flesh to give you a decent sized hollow in the middle. Take care not to pierce through the base. Cut flesh into cubes. Peel root vegetables and cut into chunks. Slice onion and celery thickly. Squash together garlic, salt and pepper. Mix cream with nutmeg and stock cube. Arrange alternating layers of vegetables in the pumpkin or marrow shell, dotting between the layers with garlic and salt mixture and butter or margarine. Pour cream and stock cube mixture over the vegetables. Place in a baking dish. Bake in a moderately slow oven for 1½-2 hours, or until flesh is softened and cooked.

Variations: Instead of cream, water may be used. If you prefer, you can cook the vegetables and pumpkin shell separately and combine just before serving.

HUNTER RATATOUILLE

Serves: 6

2 tablespoons olive oil
2 cloves garlic, crushed
500 g (1 lb) aubergine, thinly sliced
1 kg (2 lb) tomatoes, thinly sliced
500 g (1 lb) courgettes, thinly sliced
4 green or red peppers, seeded and
    thinly sliced
salt and pepper
½ bottle dry white wine

Heat oil and garlic in a large frying pan and brown the vegetables in turn, cooking quickly and transferring to a deep, heavy saucepan or flameproof casserole when browned. When all are done, pour oil from frying pan over them, season with salt and pepper, pour in the wine and simmer over a low heat for 1 hour. Do not stir. Serve hot as a vegetable accompaniment to meat or cold as an hors d'oeuvre, with white or red wine.

Note: Hunter Ratatouille can also be cooked in a lidded casserole dish in a moderately slow oven for ½-1 hour or until tender.

This dish is an ideal way to use up leftover half bottles of dry white wine, but any full-flavoured white wine will do.

STUFFED MARROW

Serves: 6
Oven temperature: moderately hot

1 large or 2 medium-sized marrows
1 onion, finely chopped
4 tablespoons butter or margarine
125 g (4 oz) mushrooms, thinly sliced
750 g (1½ lb) lean steak, minced
1 tablespoon chopped chives
1 tablespoon chopped parsley
125 g (4 oz) soft white breadcrumbs
freshly ground black pepper
salt
1 egg
1 cup tomato juice or tomato soup

Peel the marrow and remove ends. Remove all the seeds from the centre with a spoon. Fry onion in butter for 2-3 minutes, add mushrooms and minced steak and cook until meat is browned. Remove from heat. Add the chives, parsley, soft white breadcrumbs and seasoning. Bind together with the egg. Pack into the hollow marrow case, replace ends and secure with cocktail sticks. Place in a greased casserole or baking dish. Pour tomato juice or soup around. Top with a lid or with buttered foil. Bake in a moderately hot oven for 1½ hours or until the marrow is soft. Serve in slices with tomato sauce from the pan poured over.

COURGETTES PROVENÇAL

Serves: 6
Oven temperature: moderate

6 courgettes
1 small onion, chopped
4 tablespoons butter or margarine
500 g (1 lb) tomatoes
90 g (3 oz) grated cheese
salt and pepper

Cut courgettes into 5 cm (2 inch) slices and fry, with onion, in heated butter or margarine for 10-15 minutes. Skin tomatoes, and cut each one into 2-3 slices. Grease an ovenproof dish and arrange a layer of tomatoes, followed by a layer of courgettes. Sprinkle between layers with grated cheese, salt and pepper. Finish with a layer of tomatoes and sprinkle top with cheese. Bake in a moderate oven for 45 minutes.

VEGETABLE CASSEROLE

Serves: 4
Oven temperature: moderate

500 g (1 lb) courgettes
3 white onions
500 g (1 lb) cooking tomatoes or use
  canned tomatoes
3 red or green peppers
6 tablespoons olive oil or other
  vegetable oil
2 teaspoons fresh chopped thyme or 1
  teaspoon dried thyme
3 tablespoons chopped parsley
2 cloves garlic (optional)
salt and pepper

Slice the courgettes finely. Peel and slice onions, or leave in chunky quarters. Peel tomatoes if desired and cut in chunks. Remove seeds from peppers and cut into slices. Heat oil in a heavy-based saucepan or ovenproof casserole. Add onions, then tomatoes, courgettes and peppers in layers, sprinkling herbs, crushed garlic and salt and pepper between each addition. Cover and cook gently for about 1 hour on top of the stove or in a moderate oven. If the casserole is too liquid when the vegetables are tender raise the heat and boil the juices down a bit. I use my bulb baster to baste the vegetables throughout the cooking as it allows me to baste without disturbing the layers of the vegetables, which are one of the charms of this dish.

LEEKS À LA GRECQUE

Serves: 6

6 medium-sized leeks
1 tablespoon fresh chopped tarragon or 1
  teaspoon dried tarragon
1 tablespoon lemon juice
1 clove garlic, crushed
1 tablespoon finely chopped parsley
1 tomato, skinned and seeded
pinch of thyme
salt
freshly ground black pepper
1 bay leaf
¼ cup olive oil
1 cup water

Cut tops off leeks, leaving 5 cm (2 inches) of green tops. Wash thoroughly to remove any grit. If leeks are large, cut into halves lengthways. Put all ingredients into a heavy saucepan or flameproof casserole. (A flat stainless steel or ceramic dish is best.) Cover, place over high heat and bring to the boil. Lower heat and simmer gently for about 30-40 minutes until leeks are tender but firm. Allow to cool, then chill.

Note: Leeks a la Grecque may also be cooked in a lidded casserole dish in a moderately slow oven for ½-1 hour or until tender.

SCALLOPED POTATOES PROVENÇAL

Serves: 6-8
Oven temperature: moderately hot

2 onions, sliced
2 tablespoons olive oil
500 g (1 lb) tomatoes, peeled and
 chopped
salt and pepper
2 cloves garlic, crushed
6 tinned anchovies
½ teaspoon chopped thyme or mixed
 herbs
1 kg (2 lb) potatoes, peeled and sliced
2 tablespoons grated Parmesan cheese,
 or Cheddar if you prefer a milder
 flavour

Fry the onions in 1 tablespoon of the olive oil until softened. Add the chopped tomatoes and salt and pepper to taste and leave to one side of the stove. Mix the garlic and mashed anchovies with the herbs and the extra tablespoon of olive oil, or use the oil from the anchovies. Add pepper to taste.

Arrange layers of potatoes in a greased baking dish with tomatoes and onions and the anchovy mixture spread between each layer. Sprinkle top with grated cheese and a few drops of oil, then cook in a moderately hot oven for about 40 minutes or until tender. There should be enough liquid in the tomatoes, but add a bit of water if the potatoes look dry near the end of cooking.

Simple and sudden

How often have you been well and truly caught out in the kitchen? You know what I mean. Those times when your hair is in rollers, the house is a mess and you haven't done the weekly shopping. Then the telephone rings! It's a frantic message that the boss is coming to dinner.

There's no need to panic, help is at hand. Reach for the can opener and you're halfway there. It's cupboard love, so resort to instant casseroles from cans, packets and the food in your freezer. Let the canning companies do most of the hard work for you. Or try a few of the ready-mixed sauces and seasonings found on supermarket shelves these days. They make casserole cooking child's play.

Some of these recipes are cooked in minutes, others take a little longer. But whichever recipe you cook you'll be in and out of the kitchen in a flash.

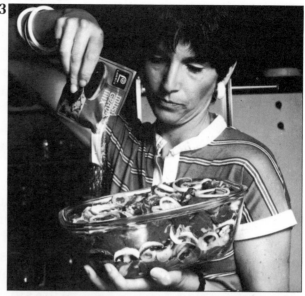

An Instant Casserole — BEEF NAOMI

Delicious casseroles are so easy with a bit of
cupboard love from packets and cans.

1 Trim stewing steak and cut into cubes.

2 Place meat in a casserole dish with alternating
layers of sliced vegetables.

3 Sprinkle between the layers with a packet of
mushroom gravy mix. Add liquid.

4 That's it! Now all you need to do is cook it. Cover
with a lid and cook in a slow oven for 1½-2 hours,
or until meat is tender.

FRENCH ONION CASSEROLE

Serves: 2-3
Oven temperature: slow

500 g (1 lb) stewing steak
1 packet French onion soup
1 can condensed cream of mushroom
  soup (about 500 g or 16 oz)
½ cup dry sherry

Cut steak into bite-sized cubes and place in a casserole dish. Mix all other ingredients in a bowl and pour over the meat. Cover and cook in a slow oven for 3 hours, or until tender. The longer and slower you cook this dish the better it will taste. This casserole can be left all day in a very slow oven, or cooked in a Crock-Pot.

BACHELOR BEEF

Serves: 2-3
Oven temperature: very slow

1 can condensed cream of mushroom
  soup (about 425 g or 15 oz)
the same can filled with water
500 g (1 lb) beef, cut into chunks
salt and pepper

Mix together all ingredients in an ovenproof dish. Top with a lid or foil and bake in a very slow oven for 2-3 hours or till tender. The longer the better as far as this recipe is concerned — it can be left in a slow oven all day or cooked in an electric slow cooker on low for 6-8 hours.

Variations: Use sherry or red wine instead of water. 125 g (4 oz) mushrooms, sliced, or whole baby ones may be added in the last 30 minutes of cooking, or add a handful of chopped shallots.

BEEF NAOMI

Serves: 4-6
Oven temperature: moderately slow

1 kg (2 lb) stewing steak
3 large onions, sliced
250 g (8 oz) mushrooms, sliced
1 packet mushroom gravy mix
garlic salt
seasoned pepper
2 cups red wine
1 cup water

Trim meat and cut into chunks. Place half the meat in a casserole dish. Top with half the onion slices and half the sliced mushrooms. Sprinkle with half the mushroom gravy mix and seasoned salt and pepper. Repeat layers using up all the meat and vegetables. Pour in wine and water. Cover and cook slowly in a moderately slow oven for 3 hours or until tender.

Variation: This dish can be made with larger quantities of meat if you like, just increase the quantities of onions and mushrooms and repeat the layers. You can make the dish with Burgundy sauce mix instead of mushroom in which case you only need water, and can leave out the wine.

PORK CHOP DELIGHT

Serves: 4
Oven temperature: moderate

4 pork chops
1 onion
1 red or green pepper
1 medium can pineapple pieces, drained
  (about 425 g or 15 oz)
1 x 440 g (15 oz) can cream of chicken or
  mushroom soup
pepper

Brown chops, onion and sliced pepper in a frying pan. Heat pineapple pieces and cream of chicken or mushroom soup separately. Arrange chops and onion in casserole dish, reserving pepper slices. Pour soup over them and season with pepper. Decorate top with pineapple pieces and pepper slices. Cover and cook in a moderate oven for 1 hour or until tender.

PORK JAMBALAYA

Serves: 4
Oven temperature: moderate

1½ cups leftover roast pork
2 rashers bacon, chopped
2 onions, sliced
1 clove garlic, crushed
2 tablespoons butter or margarine
¼ cup dry white wine
1 x 425 g (15 oz) can tomatoes or 1½ cups
　fresh, chopped tomatoes
1 tablespoon tomato paste
½ teaspoon thyme
¼ teaspoon basil
¼ teaspoon paprika
2 drops Tabasco sauce
2 teaspoons salt
freshly ground black pepper
½ teaspoon sugar
1 cup rice
1¼ cups hot water

Trim rind and most of fat from pork before cutting into cubes and measuring. Fry bacon in a frying pan until almost crisp, then add onion, garlic and butter or margarine. Cover pan with lid and cook until onion is soft. Stir in wine, tomatoes, tomato paste, herbs, paprika, Tabasco sauce, salt, pepper and sugar. Cook for 2 minutes, then stir in rice, hot water and pork. Stir well to blend, bring to the boil, then cover tightly, reduce heat and simmer, stirring occasionally, for 25 minutes; or transfer to a casserole dish, top with a lid and cook in a moderate oven 15-20 minutes. Serve immediately with a freshly cooked green vegetable or a tossed salad.

SIMPLY SNAGGERS

Serves: 2-3
Oven temperature: moderate

2 large onions, sliced thickly
1 teaspoon dried thyme
500 g (1 lb) tomatoes, chopped, or use
　equal quantity of canned tomatoes
salt and pepper
500 g (1 lb) pork sausages

Line a shallow casserole with sliced onions and sprinkle them with thyme. Add all the tomatoes and season with salt and pepper. Cover with the sausages in a single layer. Cover with a lid or with foil and bake in a moderate oven for 45-60 minutes. Remove lid for the last 10 minutes of cooking to brown sausages.

SHEPHERD'S PIE

Serves: 4-6
Oven temperature: moderately hot

1 onion
6 tablespoons butter or margarine
500 g (1 lb) cooked beef, minced
1 cup beef stock (see page 154) or water
　and beef stock cube
1 tablespoon Worcestershire sauce
1 tablespoon chopped parsley
1 tablespoon tomato ketchup
1 tablespoon fruit chutney
salt and freshly ground black pepper
4 tablespoons double cream
2 cups hot mashed potato

Chop onion and fry in 2 tablespoons of the butter or margarine until softened. Add the minced beef, stock, Worcestershire sauce, parsley, tomato ketchup, fruit chutney and salt and pepper to taste, mixing together thoroughly. Add cream and remaining butter or margarine to mashed potato, season with more salt and pepper and blend together. Place meat mixture in a greased ovenproof casserole, spread mashed potato over the top and bake for 15-20 minutes in a moderately hot oven until potato is golden brown.

PORK SAVOY

Serves: 2-3
Oven temperature: moderate

½ cup finely chopped spring onions
½ cup sliced canned mushrooms
1 tablespoon butter or margarine
500 g (1 lb) sliced cooked pork
¼ cup dry white wine
½ teaspoon crushed black peppercorns
1 x 440 g (15 oz) can cream of mushroom
  soup

Fry spring onions and mushrooms in a flameproof casserole dish in butter or margarine. Place pork on top, add white wine and sprinkle with black peppercorns. Add cream of mushroom soup and slowly bring to the boil. Simmer for 10-15 minutes or in a moderate oven for 15-20 minutes.

BUSY BIRD CHICKEN

Serves: 4
Oven temperature: moderately slow

1 chicken, cut into joints (see page 42)
salt and pepper
1 packet French onion soup
1 small knob green root ginger, finely
  sliced
1 medium can apricot juice (about 425 g
  or 15 oz)
2-4 teaspoons cornflour
2 tablespoons cold water
½ cup sliced almonds, toasted

Place chicken pieces in a heavy casserole dish. Sprinkle well with salt, pepper and French onion soup, scattering slices of ginger between chicken. Pour apricot juice over the chicken. Top with a lid and cook in a moderately slow oven for 2 hours or till tender. If necessary, thicken sauce with cornflour mixed to a cream with cold water and simmer a few minutes after adding to the juices. Just before serving scatter toasted sliced almonds over the top. Serve with fried brown rice cooked with a little garlic.

BEEF AND VEGETABLE STEW

Serves: 2-4
Oven temperature: moderately slow

500 g (1 lb) chuck steak
plain flour
1 onion, chopped
1 carrot, chopped
1 stick celery, chopped
2-3 peeled and chopped potatoes
1 x 865 g (28 oz) can beef vegetable soup
2 beef stock cubes
salt and pepper
pinch mixed herbs

Cut meat into chunks, toss in flour and place in casserole dish, with chopped vegetables on top. Add can of soup and crushed stock cubes. Add salt and pepper to taste, with a pinch of mixed herbs. Cook in a moderate oven till meat is tender. Serve hot.

Note: This basic recipe can be varied by substituting or adding different vegetables — perhaps even leftovers.

HAWAIIAN BEEF VEGETABLE

Serves: 2
Oven temperature: moderate

1 x 865 g (28 oz) can beef vegetable soup
1 beef stock cube
1 can crushed pineapple (about 425 g or
   15 oz)
1 packet chicken noodle soup
1 teaspoon soy sauce
250 g (8 oz) beef, cut into chunks
½ cabbage, shredded

Place all the ingredients except the cabbage into a large casserole dish. Spread shredded cabbage over top, cover with a lid and place in moderate oven for 45 minutes or until meat is tender.

SUCCOTASH

Serves: 2-4
Oven temperature: moderate

500 g (1 lb) canned baby lima beans
500 g (1 lb) canned corn kernels
1 green pepper, sliced
salt and pepper
2-4 tablespoons butter or margarine
chopped parsley or paprika to garnish

Combine all ingredients except garnish in a saucepan or casserole dish. Cook very gently, covered, on top of the stove or in a moderate oven for about 10 minutes, until vegetables are cooked and soft, but not soggy. Add more salt and pepper to taste. Sprinkle with chopped parsley or paprika just before serving.

SAVOURY SPAGHETTI

Serves: 2-3
Oven temperature: moderate

500 g (1 lb) minced steak
½ cup onion, chopped
1 clove garlic, crushed
½ cup chopped green pepper
2 tablespoons butter or margarine
1 x 865 g (28 oz) can minestrone soup
250 g (8 oz) spaghetti, cooked and
   drained
1 cup grated cheese

Cook mince, onion, garlic and pepper in the butter or margarine in a frying pan till lightly brown. Add minestrone soup and heat till nearly boiling. Add spaghetti and half the cheese and pour into a casserole. Top with remaining cheese, cover with a lid, and cook in moderate oven about 30 minutes.

CELERY CHICKEN CASSEROLE

Serves: 4
Oven temperature: moderate

2 cups shredded leftover chicken
1 x 865 g (28 oz) can chicken and
   vegetable soup
½ cup chopped celery
1 red pepper, chopped
1 onion, diced

Place chicken in casserole dish. Mix together chicken and vegetable soup, celery, capsicum and onion. Pour over chicken, cover, and cook in a moderate oven for 10-20 minutes till heated through. Serve with boiled rice.

Switched-on casseroles

Grandma would have called her 'fast', the twentieth-century girl of today, who gallivants away from the house for hours on end, working at a full-time job instead of spending her time chained to the stove.

Sure, she's switched on. She gets her charge from power-point cooking, and those modern-day marvels, electric kitchen aids. And why not? There are so many power-point gadgets around these days.

However, Granny wouldn't complain about the flavour of the bubbling food. Casserole cooking in slow cooking electric appliances is the next best thing to cooking on a wood stove, with its long slow simmering throughout the day. And pressure cookers make casserole cooking an almost instant affair.

ELECTRIC SLOW COOKER

There's no doubt about it, there's something extra special about food that has been gently simmering all day long. Now we can achieve wood-stove flavour with the electric slow cooker.

It's so simple: tip the food into the pot, switch it on and forget about it. Let it cook the dinner gently during the night or all through the day — 8 to 10 hours later it will be ready to serve.

The only difference between the casserole recipes in this chapter and those in the other chapters of the book is the quantity of liquid used. Slow cookers need much less liquid, because the food releases a lot of its own juices. So, if you wish to adapt any casserole recipe for slow cooking, simply reduce the quantity of the liquid.

VEAL IN A CREAM SAUCE

Serves: 6
Oven Temperature: Moderate

1.5 kg (3 lbs) veal shoulder, boned
8 small onions
4 small carrots, quartered
1 bay leaf
pinch dried thyme
2 sprigs parsley
2 teaspoons salt
ground pepper
1 cup white wine

Sauce:
2 tablespoons butter or margarine
2 tablespoons flour
½ cup cream
1 egg yolk
1 tablespoon lemon juice
chopped parsley to garnish.

Cut veal into good sized pieces. Place in electric slow cooker or casserole dish with remaining ingredients. Cover and cook on high for 3-4 hours or low for 8-10 hours. Strain and retain stock, when cooked and tender. This can also be cooked on top of the stove or in a moderate oven for 1-1½ hours or till tender. Strain and retain stock.

Sauce: Make a sauce in a separate pan. Melt butter or margarine and stir in flour. Slowly add 2 cups of the veal stock and cook gently over a medium heat. Whisk ½ cup of cream with the egg yolk. Slowly stir in some of the hot sauce then pour the egg mixture back into the sauce. Season with 1 tablespoon of lemon juice, salt and pepper. Pour sauce over veal in slow cooker, casserole dish or on top of the stove and reheat on low for about 10 minutes, or return to the boil or reheat in the oven. Sprinkle over a little parsley. Serve with boiled rice.

BEAN SOUP

Serves: 8

500 g (1 lb) dry kidney beans (soaked
    overnight)
6 cups water
1-2 cups tomato juice
500 g (1 lb) meaty ham bones or ham
    pieces
1 teaspoon salt
5 whole peppercorns or ½ teaspoon
    pepper
½ cup celery leaves, chopped
1 medium onion, chopped
1 bay leaf

Put all ingredients in the electric slow cooker or casserole
dish. Cover and cook on low for 10-12 hours, or till beans
are tender. If desired this may also be simmered on top of
the stove or cooked in a casserole dish in a moderate oven
for 2 hours or till the beans are tender. Remove bones and
chop up ham into small pieces. Return to soup. Serve with
crusty French bread.

HAWAIIAN CHICKEN

Serves: 6-8

2 tablespoons vegetable oil
6-8 chicken portions
1 onion, chopped
500 g (1 lb) courgettes, trimmed and
    sliced
1 x 198 g (7 oz) can pineapple slices
½ cup chicken stock (see page 154) or
    water and stock cubes
1 tablespoon soy sauce
1 tablespoon tomato paste
salt and freshly ground pepper
2 teaspoons cornflour
juice of 1 small orange

Heat oil in a frying pan and cook chicken for 10 minutes
until golden brown. Remove chicken pieces from pan and
place in electric slow cooker or casserole dish. Add onion
and courgettes to the frying pan and cook till softened. Mix
the pineapple syrup, stock, soy sauce, tomato paste, salt
and pepper and cornflour with the orange juice and mix
thoroughly to make a smooth paste. Add to the pan and
bring to the boil. Stir well.

Place a pineapple slice on each chicken piece. Pour over the
sauce, top with a lid and cook on high for 3-4 hours, or low
for 6-8 hours. If cooking on top of the stove or in the oven,
add ½ cup more chicken stock or water. Simmer gently on
top of the stove for 50-60 minutes or cook in a moderate
oven for 1-1¼ hours or till tender.

CARIBBEAN LAMB

Serves: 4-6
Oven temperature: moderate

1 kg (2 lb) breast of lamb
2 tablespoons vegetable oil
1 sliced onion
1 clove garlic, crushed
1 teaspoon dry mustard
¼ teaspoon ground ginger
pinch cayenne pepper
2 teaspoons sugar
2 tablespoons tomato paste
2 tablespoons Worcestershire sauce
1 tablespoon vinegar
1 x 250 g (8 oz) can pineapple pieces.

Trim any excess fat from the lamb and cut meat into
pieces, between the ribs. Heat the oil in a frying pan and
fry the meat for about 10 minutes until browned. Drain
and serve.
    Add the onion and garlic to the frying pan and fry for
about 5 minutes till softened. Add seasonings, sugar,
tomato paste, Worcestershire sauce, vinegar and pineapple
pieces with the juice. Bring to the boil, stirring to combine
well. Transfer to the electric slow cooker or casserole dish
with the meat, top with a lid and cook on high for 6-8
hours. If cooking on top of the stove or in the oven, then
add 1 cup more liquid (either water or wine). Simmer
gently for 1½-2 hours, or cook in a moderate oven for 1½-2
hours or till tender.

CREAMY POT ROAST

Serves: 8-10
Oven Temperature: Moderately slow

2-2.5 kg (4-5 lbs) chuck, topside or
   rump roast beef
1 clove garlic
salt and pepper
1 chopped carrot
1 stalk celery, chopped
1 small onion, stuck with 3 cloves
¾ cup sour cream mixed with 3
   tablespoons flour.

Rub the beef roast all over with garlic and season well with salt and pepper. Place in electric slow cooker or casserole dish and add all the remaining ingredients. Cover and cook on low for 10-12 hours or top with a lid and cook in a moderately slow oven for 2-2½ hours or till tender. It may be necessary to add 1 cup extra sour cream if the mixture seems to dry out. This is beautiful served either hot or cold. Serve with buttery noodles.

MUSHROOM CHICKEN

Serves: 4-6 people
Oven Temperature: moderate

3 tablespoons butter or margarine
2 onions, chopped
4 rashers chopped bacon
6 chicken pieces frozen and thawed
1 packet dry mushroom soup
¼ cup sherry or white wine
1 crumbled chicken stock cube
pinch tarragon
125 g (4 oz) fresh sliced mushrooms,
   or 1 can sliced mushrooms
¼ cup sour cream

Melt the butter or margarine. Add chopped bacon and onion and cook till softened. Remove bacon and onion and place in a casserole dish or electric slow cooker.

Add chicken pieces to the frying pan and fry till golden brown, then place in the casserole dish or electric slow cooker. Sprinkle dry mushroom soup and crumbled stock cube over the top. Add pinch tarragon, sherry or wine. If cooking in a casserole in the oven, or on top of stove, add 1 cup more sherry or wine, or water.

Add mushrooms and sour cream to pot, stir well. Cover and cook in an electric slow cooker on high for 8-10 hours or — cook in a moderate oven for 1-1¼ hours or till tender — or simmer on top of the stove for 50-60 minutes. Serve with either rice or noodles.

STEAK AND KIDNEY A LA KING

Serves: 4-6
Oven temperature: very slow
Electric slow cooker

1 kg (2 lb) stewing beef
250 g (8 oz) kidneys
1 packet Burgundy sauce mix
1 red cabbage

Trim meat and kidneys removing all fat and gristle. Cut into chunks. Place in an electric slow cooker. Sprinkle with sauce mix and stir. Chop red cabbage and place on top of the beef. This recipe needs no liquid. Top with a lid and cook on low for 8-10 hours, or you can cook this recipe in a lidded casserole dish in a very slow oven for 4-5 hours. Serve the cabbage either stirred through the steak and kidney or in a separate dish.

TRIPE À LA MODE

Serves: 10-12
Electric slow cooker

6 medium-sized onions, sliced
6 medium-sized carrots, sliced
1 calf's foot
**2.5 kg (5 lb) tripe, cleaned and cut into
    2.5 cm (1 inch) pieces**
1 bouquet garni (see page 82)
4 leeks, washed
4 cloves garlic, cut in halves
2 teaspoons salt
1 teaspoon pepper
½ teaspoon allspice
500 g (1 lb) fatty beef
**cider and water, combined in equal
    quantities, to cover**
½ cup Calvados or brandy

Line the base of an electric slow cooker or heavy based ovenproof casserole with onion and carrot. Remove bone and cut calf's foot into 2-3 pieces. Place in pot with the bone. Add tripe, bouquet garni, leeks, garlic, salt, pepper and allspice. Slice beef fat and cover tripe. Add combined cider and water to cover and Calvados or brandy.

Cover and cook in slow cooker on low, or in a very very slow oven for 10-12 hours (it is a good idea to cook it overnight). Skim off fat. Discard calf's foot, leeks, bouquet garni and vegetables. Place tripe in a large serving dish and strain liquid over, removing any surplus fat. If preferred, after removing calf's foot and vegetables, allow casserole to cool and remove fat when it sets on the surface. Reheat tripe and liquid and serve very hot.

BRAISED BEEF MAMAN

Serves: 4-6
Oven temperature: moderately slow
Electric slow cooker

1 kg (2 lb) slab topside steak, cut thick
3-4 tablespoons plain flour
salt and pepper
4 tablespoons beef dripping
1 clove garlic, crushed
¾ cup dry sherry
1 bay leaf

Trim fat from steak and chop into bite-sized chunks. Toss in seasoned flour and fry in hot dripping with garlic till well browned on all sides. Remove from heat and add sherry. (Watch out for spitting fat.) Stir well scraping up the crusty bits and pieces in the pan. Transfer meat and pan juices to electric slow cooker and add bay leaf. Cover and cook on low for 6-8 hours. You can also cook this recipe in a pressure cooker for just 15-20 minutes or in a lidded casserole dish in a moderately slow oven for 1½-2 hours or till tender. Serve with fried rice.

Variation: This recipe may be varied by adding sliced onions and green pepper or by using red wine instead of sherry.

SHERRY CHICKEN

Serves: 8
Oven temperature: slow
Electric slow cooker

2 chickens
1 tablespoon paprika
1 teaspoon ground black pepper
½ cup oil
2 onions, chopped
**½ cup dry sherry (or 1 cup if oven
    cooking)**
¼ cup soy sauce
**1 cup canned, peeled tomatoes, or 3
    tomatoes, peeled and cut into chunks**
1 tablespoon tomato paste
2 tablespoons sesame seeds
1-2 cloves garlic, crushed
salt

Cut chicken into pieces (see page 46). Mix together paprika and pepper and toss chicken in this mixture. Heat oil in a frying pan and fry chicken pieces until browned and crisp. Remove and place in an electric slow cooker or a casserole dish. Add chopped onion to the frying pan and fry until softened. Remove and add to the chicken. Add dry sherry and soy sauce to the frying pan and stir to remove the bits and pieces from the bottom of the pan. If using a slow cooker, strain the tomatoes and discard juice, but retain juice if cooking in the oven. Add all other ingredients to tomatoes and mix well. Pour over the chicken, stir well and cover. Cook for 6-8 hours on low or in a slow oven for 1½-2 hours.

JAN'S GOULASH

Serves: 3-4
Oven temperature: slow
Electric slow cooker

750 g (1½ lb) lean stewing beef
3 tablespoons butter or margarine
6 onions, sliced
2 cloves garlic, crushed
1½ tablespoons paprika
1 tablespoon plain flour
salt
freshly ground pepper
2 teaspoons caraway seeds (optional)
1 teaspoon dried marjoram or mixed
    herbs
1 tablespoon tomato paste
4 large prunes, stoned and chopped
½ cup water
1 crumbled beef stock cube
2 tablespoons yoghurt

Remove the fat, gristle and skin from the meat and cut it into chunks. Melt butter or margarine in a frying pan and fry the onions and garlic until the onions are softened. Add meat and cook until brown. Sprinkle with paprika and flour. Stir and cook for a few minutes and then remove from the heat. Transfer the mixture to an electric slow cooker or casserole dish. Add seasonings, caraway seeds if used, marjoram or mixed herbs, tomato paste, prunes, water and stock cube. If cooking in a casserole in the oven add 1 cup more water. Mix well. Cover and cook in a slow cooker for 8-10 hours on low or in a slow oven for 2-3 hours. Just before serving stir in the yoghurt. Serve with buttery boiled potatoes.

Note: If freezing this dish, do not add yoghurt until thawed and reheated.

BEEF CATALAN

Serves: 4-6
Oven temperature: slow
Electric slow cooker

4 rashers bacon
1 kg (2 lb) topside or stewing steak
2 onions, sliced
2 carrots, sliced
½ cup sliced mushrooms
1 clove garlic, crushed
pinch nutmeg
1 teaspoon thyme
1 tablespoon butter or margarine
salt and pepper
1 can tomatoes (about 425 g or 15 oz)
1 tablespoon black treacle or golden
    syrup
½ cup red wine
1 tablespoon brandy (optional)

Fry bacon until fat runs. Fry meat in the bacon fat until brown on all sides. Place in slow cooker with all other ingredients and cook 8-10 hours or till tender. This would need 2-3 hours slow cooking on top of the stove or in a slow oven.

Background: Crock-Pot *Silverside* and Beans (page 127);
foreground: French Seafood (page 133)

BEERY BEEF

Serves: 4-6
Oven temperature: slow
Electric slow cooker

1 kg (2 lb) topside or stewing steak
salt and pepper
4 tablespoons butter, margarine or
    dripping
3 rashers bacon, thickly sliced
4 onions, sliced
1½ tablespoons plain flour
1 cup beer (2 cups beer if oven cooking)
1 tablespoon vinegar
2 cloves garlic, crushed
2 tablespoons brown sugar
1 bay leaf
1 teaspoon dried thyme
2 tablespoons chopped parsley

Cut the meat into big chunks and season well with salt and pepper. Heat 3 tablespoons of the fat in a frying pan, add the meat and fry until brown. Add the chopped bacon and cook until fat is transparent. Remove beef and bacon from the pan. Add onions and fry until tender, then remove. Pour off surplus fat and add 1 tablespoon extra butter, margarine or dripping. Add flour and stir to combine. Remove from the heat, add beer and vinegar, stirring to combine. (Remember that if you are cooking in the oven, not in in an electric slow cooker, you need 2 cups of beer). Return to heat and bring to the boil to thicken. Add garlic, sugar and herbs. Arrange alternate layers of meat and onion in an electric slow cooker or a casserole dish. Pour the sauce over layers. Cover and cook in an electric slow cooker on low for 8-10 hours or until tender, or cook in a slow oven for about 3 hours, or until meat is tender. Skim off any fat from the surface.

Note: This dish is best made the day before serving.

SILVERSIDE AND BEANS

Serves: 4-6
Electric slow cooker or pressure cooker

2 kg (4 lb) piece silverside
250 g (8 oz) dried chick peas, or other
    dried beans
2 large carrots
2 large onions or 6 tiny ones
1 can whole tomatoes (about 425 g or
    15oz)
4 tablespoons brown sugar
pepper
1 bay leaf
1 cup water
1 cup white wine or cider
1-2 potatoes, sliced
1 can apricot halves (about 425 g or 15
    oz)
1 cup frozen peas (optional)

Check with your butcher and if the meat is very salty, soak in cold water for at least 1 hour to remove excess salt. Soak dried peas or beans in cold water overnight. Drain beef and the peas or beans. Peel carrots and cut into big chunks. Peel onions and if large cut into quarters. Place meat in an electric slow cooker, add soaked peas or beans and other vegetables then add canned tomatoes with their juice, 2 tablespoons of the brown sugar, pepper, bay leaf, water and wine or cider. Cook on high for 8-10 hours. If cooking this recipe on top of the stove, bring to the boil, cover, turn heat very low and simmer for 2½-3 hours; or cook in a pressure cooker for 1 hour.

Halfway through the cooking, check the flavour of the vegetable mixture and beef. If the sauce is becoming too salty, remove the meat and put it into another saucepan with 1-2 potatoes and water to cover. Continue cooking separately till tender. If not too salty then continue cooking in the same pot, checking flavour occasionally. Whether or not you have to remove the meat continue cooking vegetables in the original pot. When meat is cooked, remove vegetables from slow cooker or pressure cooker, with the liquid and place in a saucepan. Bring to the boil and cook rapidly until liquid thickens. If using frozen peas, add them at this stage.

To finish off the beef, put drained meat in an oven dish and top with apricot halves. Sprinkle with remaining 2 tablespoons of brown sugar and flash cook in a hot oven until meat is heated and sugar melts to a golden brown glaze (about 15-20 minutes).

Chicken with Cider (page 52)

PRESSURE COOKER

When using your pressure cooker, always be
guided by the manufacturer's instructions.
Whatever the model, the various steps must be
carried out in the right order — for example,
food is fried without the lid on, meat and
vegetables should not fill the pan more than
two thirds — before the lid goes on. The liquid
in the cooker (it should never be less than
300ml/10 fl oz) is brought to the boil to create
steam that drives the air from the pan. When a
loud hiss indicates that the pressure in the
cooker has been reached (most casseroles are
cooked at high pressure), reduce the heat and
start timing from when the hiss becomes a
gentle, steady 'muttering'. This 'mutter' should
be maintained over low heat throughout the
cooking time. Reduce pressure by placing the
cooker under cold running water.

If there is too much liquid in the casserole at
the end of the cooking time, boil rapidly
without the lid to reduce it; or stir in a
thickening agent and cook without the lid until
thickened. When vegetables have to be added
towards the end of the cooking time, reduce
pressure, remove lid, add vegetables and cook
without the lid.

MUTTON WITH BEANS

Serves: 4-6
Pressure cooker

**250 g (8 oz) dried beans, kidney, haricot
or lima**
**1 kg (2 lb) lamb or mutton neck chops, or
breast of lamb cut into slices**
2 tablespoons oil or dripping
2 onions, chopped
1 turnip, chopped
2 carrots, chopped
1 clove garlic, crushed
1 teaspoon mixed herbs
1 teaspoon Worcestershire sauce
2 tablespoons tomato ketchup
salt and pepper

Soak beans in water overnight. Brown the meat in oil or
dripping. Remove meat, add vegetables and garlic to the
pot and fry till slightly browned and softened. Return
meat to pot with beans and enough water to just cover.
Add all other ingredients and bring up to pressure. Turn
down heat and gently cook for 45 minutes or until
beans are tender. If cooking the normal way then simmer
for 1½-2 hours.

LIN'S STEAMED CHICKEN

Serves: 4
Oven temperature: moderately slow
Pressure cooker

1 x 1.5 kg (3 lb) chicken
1 packet vegetable soup (or fresh
    chopped turnip, parsnip, onion,
    celery and a potato)
2 carrots, chopped
2 courgettes, sliced
2 tomatoes, cores removed and left
    whole
2 leeks (optional)
salt
freshly ground pepper
1-2 sprigs parsley

Place chicken in a pressure cooker. Add all remaining ingredients plus water to almost cover the bird and season with salt, pepper and parsley. Bring up to pressure and cook for 15-20 minutes or till tender. If not cooking under pressure simmer gently in a saucepan for about 1 hour. This recipe can also be cooked in a lidded casserole dish in a moderately slow oven for 1-1½ hours or till tender.

When tender remove chicken and vegetables to a plate and serve.

Variation: You can make this recipe extra special with the following sauce. Cook 4 tablespoons butter with 4 tablespoons flour until bubbly and combined. Off the heat add about a cup of the stock from the chicken and ¼ cup white wine. Stir well then bring to the boil and simmer a few minutes. Add ¼ cup milk or cream and serve in a gravy boat with the steamed chicken.

Note: The stock from this recipe makes very good jellied stock, a good base for lettuce soup.

If freezing cut the chicken into joints after cooking. The rest of the recipe stays the same, but if you are making the sauce cut out the milk or cream.

The vegetables for this recipe may be varied according to what you have in the refrigerator.

POT ROAST DELUXE

Serves: 10-12
Pressure cooker

1 kg (2 lb) potatoes
2 onions
3 tablespoons oil
2 rashers of bacon, diced
3 cloves garlic
paprika
basil
oregano
marjoram
thyme
1 bay leaf, crumbled
salt and pepper
2 kg (4 lb) brisket of beef
1 pig's knuckle
3 carrots
2 tablespoons brown sugar
2 cups red wine

Peel potatoes and slice. Chop onions. Fry potatoes and onions in oil with bacon and garlic until softened and slightly browned then remove from pan. Mix together spices and rub all over the meat. Brown meat in remaining fat in pan, on all sides. Place all ingredients in the pressure cooker and cook gently for 1 hour or till tender (3-4 hours of normal cooking).

This recipe requires a very large pressure cooker. In a smaller pressure cooker, Pot Roast Deluxe can be made to serve 8 by using 1.5 (3lb) brisket of beef, and the other ingredients as listed. Cook for 45 minutes.

BEEF CITRON

Serves: 4-6
Pressure cooker

1 kg (2 lb) stewing steak
plain flour to coat beef
salt and pepper
2 tablespoons oil or dripping
500 g (1 lb) carrots, sliced
2 onions, chopped
1 green pepper, sliced
1 clove garlic, crushed
1 teaspoon dried or freshly chopped
   thyme
juice and rind 1 orange
1 cup white wine, water, or sherry or
   vermouth mixed with water
1 teaspoon brown sugar

Trim meat, cut into cubes and toss in flour mixed with salt and pepper. Fry in hot oil or dripping until browned. Remove. Add vegetables and fry until browned. Return meat to the pan and add all other ingredients. Bring up to pressure and cook gently for 20-25 minutes or until tender (or simmer for 1-1½ hours on top of stove). Serve with fried rice or buttery noodles.

EASY OXTAIL

Serves: 6-8
Oven temperature: moderately slow
Pressure cooker

1 kg (2 lb) oxtail
2 tablespoons cooking oil
1 x 140 g (4½ oz) can tomato paste
3 carrots
3 leeks
3 onions
salt and pepper
5 cups water
1 x 440 g (15 oz) can condensed oxtail
   soup

Cut oxtail into small chunks. Heat oil in pressure cooker or a large saucepan, add oxtail and stir until meat browns. Blend in the tomato paste. Clean and dice vegetables and add to pan, along with salt and pepper. Reheat, stirring constantly. Add the water and oxtail soup, bring to the boil, cover and pressure cook for 45-60 minutes, or simmer on top of the stove or in a moderately slow oven for 1-2 hours, until tender.

SPICY BEEF STEW

Serves: 4-6
Pressure cooker

1 kg (2 lb) chuck steak
2 tablespoons oil
3 onions, sliced
2-3 cloves garlic, crushed
1 teaspoon cinnamon
1 teaspoon ground cardamom, or 2
   teaspoons cardamom seeds or pods, or
   1 teaspoon curry powder
3 cloves
500 g (1 lb) carrots, chopped
3 potatoes, peeled and chopped
2 tomatoes, chopped
salt and pepper
1 cup water or tomato juice
½ cauliflower

Trim meat and cut into chunks. Fry in oil until browned on all sides. Remove. Add onions, garlic, cinnamon, cardamom or curry powder and fry until softened. Return meat to the pan and add all other ingredients except cauliflower. Bring up to pressure and cook gently for 20 minutes or for 1 hour normal cooking. Open pressure cooker and add cauliflower pieces. Cook for a further 5 minutes. If necessary boil to thicken the sauce, or thicken with 1-2 teaspoons cornflour.

BOSTON BAKED BEANS

Serves: 6-8
Pressure cooker

1½ cups dried beans
1 onion, chopped
2 tablespoons dark treacle
3 tablespoons tomato ketchup
1 tablespoon dry mustard
salt
½ cup water or beer
1 teaspoon vinegar
1 cup sliced salt pork
1 tablespoon Worcestershire sauce

Soak beans in cold water overnight. Place in pressure cooker with chopped onion and water to just cover. Bring up to pressure and cook gently for 30-45 minutes or until tender or simmer on top of stove for 1½-2 hours. Drain, add other ingredients, return to pressure and cook gently for a further 10-20 minutes (or 45-60 minutes normal cooking).

ELECTRIC FRY PAN

Although the electric fry pan is not a newcomer to the kitchen, it is still a useful appliance. I find it is a bit shallow for true casserole cooking, and the liquid does boil away if you're not careful. This is easily rectified, however, by increasing the amount of liquid in the recipe. On the other hand, if a recipe calls for reducing the liquid and boiling it away by half, then, of course, a fry pan is ideal.

SPECIAL TACOS

Serves: 12
Electric frypan

Tacos
1 onion, finely chopped
2 tablespoons oil
1 kg (2 lb) minced steak
½ cup tomato juice
1 packet commercial taco sauce
1 x 450 g (1 lb) can beans in chilli sauce
salt and pepper

Garnishes
taco shells or split hamburger rolls
1 onion, chopped
2 tomatoes, chopped
½ lettuce, shredded
250 g (8 oz) grated cheese
½ cup olives

Fry onions in hot oil in frypan until softened. Add minced steak and fry till brown. Pour off excess fat and add all other ingredients. Stir well. Simmer for 25-35 minutes or until cooked and flavours are well combined.

To serve: Place the pot of meat sauce on the table and surround with bowls of the different garnishes. Fill taco shells or split hamburger rolls with meat sauce then sprinkle with a choice of garnishes. This is a great dish for entertaining as everyone can help themselves.

Note: Special Taco's may also be cooked in an electric slow cooker on high for 6 hours.

BEEF ON THE BOIL

Serves: 8-10
Electric frypan

500 g (1 lb) chicken giblets
1.5 kg (3 lb) boneless piece of beef —
  chuck or unsalted silverside
1½ teaspoons salt
4 tablespoons butter or margarine
2 onions, thickly sliced
2 carrots, thickly sliced
2 stalks celery, cut into pieces
1 leek, cut into pieces
5 sprigs parsley
1 bay leaf
6 peppercorns
4 whole allspice, or ½ teaspoon
  powdered allspice

Place the chicken giblets in an electric frypan or a large pot, place the beef on top and just cover with water. Add salt and bring to the boil. Skim off the fat. Heat butter or margarine in a frying pan, add onion, carrot, celery and leek, then toss over a high heat until lightly coloured and softened. Add the vegetables to the meat with the parsley, bay leaf, peppercorns and allspice. Bring to boil and turn the heat down low, and cover the frypan or saucepan with a lid. Simmer very, very slowly until the beef is tender, for about 2½ hours. To serve, remove meat and cut into thick slices. Skim surface fat from the stock, then strain through a sieve. Push vegetables through the sieve, or put them in the blender. The resulting puree should be moistened with a little of the stock to form a sauce. Pour this over the beef slices.

This dish is delicious eaten with boiled potatoes or noodles, with a side salad.

Note: Beef on the Boil may also be cooked in a lidded casserole dish in a moderately slow oven for 1½-2 hours or until tender. You can serve the leftover stock as a soup with dumplings (see page 156) in it.

CHILLI CON CARNE

Serves: 4-5
Electric frypan

2 tablespoons oil
2 onions, finely chopped
750 g (1½ lb) minced beef
1 clove garlic, crushed
salt and pepper
1 teaspoon chilli powder or to taste
1 teaspoon oregano
1 cup tomato purée or ¼ cup tomato
**   paste**
1 cup hot water
1 chicken stock cube
1 can red kidney beans, drained (about
**   425 g or 15 oz)**

Heat oil in electric frypan. Add onions and cook over low heat until softened, then remove them to a plate. Add meat to the pan and fry until browned, adding more oil if necessary. Add garlic, salt and pepper, chilli powder and oregano and cook for 1-2 minutes. Return onions to the pan, add all other ingredients except beans and simmer for 20 minutes. Just before serving stir in beans and cook another 10 minutes to heat. Serve with crusty bread and a green salad.

FRENCH SEAFOOD

Serves: 8-10
Electric frypan

2 kg (4 lb) fresh fish and seafood
¼ cup oil
1 onion, chopped
1 leek sliced, or 1 bunch spring
**   onions, chopped**
3-4 cups fish stock (see page 154)
4 tomatoes
4 cloves garlic
grated rind and juice of 1 lemon
1 teaspoon grated orange rind
2 tablespoons tomato paste
3 tablespoons chopped parsley
2 teaspoons fresh dill or fennel
salt and freshly ground pepper

The fish you use depends on the markets, the season and your budget, but try to get a combination of some of the following: mullet, cod, halibut, haddock, bream, lobster, prawns, scallops, mussels or squid. Prepare the seafood by removing skin and heads from fish to make stock. Scrub mussels, remove shells from shellfish and use these and heads for stock. Cut fish flesh into bite-sized pieces.

Heat oil in an electric frypan and add onion, leek or spring onions and fry until softened. Add all remaining ingredients, except seafood, and bring to the boil. Simmer 5 minutes. Add seafood and simmer until cooked. Do this in batches, beginning with the slowest cooking pieces and leaving the shellfish until the end as it takes only about 5 minutes. Check soup for salf and pepper and serve with chunks of crusty French bread.

SWEDISH ON THE BALL

Serves: 3-4
Electric frypan

¼ cup chopped onion
1 tablespoon butter or margarine
500 g (1 lb) minced veal and pork
¼ teaspoon salt
dash white pepper
2 tablespoons plain flour
1 egg
¼ cup double cream
1 x 865 g (28 oz) can beef and
**   vegetable soup**

Cook onion in butter or margarine till tender, but not brown in an electric frypan. Combine meats and seasonings and beat thoroughly. Add in flour, then egg and gradually beat in cream. Add cooked onion. Form mixture into 24 balls and lightly brown them in a little additional butter or margarine in the frypan. Remove excess fat. Add beef and vegetable soup and cook, uncovered, for 12-15 minutes.

CHICKEN AND VEGETABLE STEW

Serves: 6-8
Electric frypan

1 x 1.5 kg (3 lb) roasting chicken
1 tablespoon butter, margarine or bacon
**   fat**
1 tablespoon oil
1 stick celery, chopped
1 onion, chopped
2 turnips or parsnips, chopped
4 carrots, chopped
3 large potatoes, peeled and sliced
2 cups water
4 chicken stock cubes
1 bay leaf
1 clove garlic, crushed
¼ cup tomato paste
¼ tablespoon each dried tarragon and
**   thyme, or ½ tablespoon mixed herbs**
½ cup white wine
frozen broccoli (optional)

Cut chicken into joints (see page 46). Heat butter. margarine or bacon fat, and oil in electric frypan or deep saucepan and add the vegetables. Fry until softened. Add chicken pieces, 2 cups water, stock cubes and all other ingredients. Cover and cook for 30 minutes or until chicken pieces are done. If desired, a bunch of frozen broccoli may be added to the dish during the last 10 minutes of cooking.

Note: Chicken and Vegetable Stew may also be cooked in a lidded casserole dish in a moderately slow oven for 15-30 minutes or until tender.

LEMON NUTMEG BEEF BALLS

Serves: 4
Electric frypan

750 g (1½ lb) minced beef
1 cup fresh breadcrumbs
3 tablespoons tomato ketchup
3 tablespoons sherry
¾ teaspoon salt
1 teaspoon celery salt
1 teaspoon grated lemon rind
½ teaspoon ground nutmeg
½ teaspoon garlic powder
oil, butter or margarine
1 x 865 g (28 oz) can beef and
**   vegetable soup**
¼ cup sour cream (optional)

Mix the first 9 ingredients together and form the mixture into balls. Brown balls over low heat in a small quantity of oil, butter or margarine in electric frypan. Add the beef and vegetable soup and bring to the boil. Lower heat and simmer 20 minutes. Stir in sour cream, if used, and add more salt to taste. Serve over rice or pasta.

BEEF BOLOGNESE

Serves: 3-4
Electric frypan

1 onion, chopped
2 tablespoons oil
2 cloves garlic, crushed
500 g (1 lb) minced meat
1 carrot, grated
1 green pepper, diced
125 g (4 oz) mushrooms, sliced
1 x 500 g (1 lb) can tomatoes
2 tablespoons tomato paste
½ cup dry white wine
½ teaspoon dried basil
1 tablespoon parsley, finely chopped
salt
freshly ground pepper
1 teaspoon brown sugar

Fry onion in the oil in electric frypan until soft.
Add garlic and minced meat and cook quickly until meat
is brown. Add carrot, pepper and mushrooms,
tomatoes, tomato paste, wine, herbs, salt, pepper and
sugar. Stir to combine, then cover with a tight lid.
Simmer the sauce gently for ¾-1 hour, stirring
occasionally.

Serve spooned over boiled spaghetti with grated
Parmesan cheese scattered over the top.

EASY CURRY

Serves: 4
Electric frypan

750 g (1½ lb) stewing steak
1 cup water
1 x 865 g (28 oz) can beef vegetable soup
1 onion, chopped
2 tablespoons oil
1½ teaspoons cummin
1½ tablespoons curry paste
1 teaspoon chilli powder
1½ teaspoons ground coriander
½ teaspoon ground nutmeg
¼ teaspoon ground cloves
2 tablespoons tomato ketchup
salt
1 cooking apple, peeled and chopped

Place beef in an electric frypan. Add water and 1½
cups of the beef and vegetable soup. Bring to boil, cover,
and simmer 1 hour or till tender. Drain meat, reserving the
broth. In the frypan, fry onion in the oil till tender.
Stir in spices, 1 cup of reserved broth and tomato ketchup
and simmer, covered, for 5 minutes. Add beef, the rest of
the cooking broth and the remainder of the can of soup and
salt to taste and simmer 15 minutes. Add apple and
simmer a further 15 minutes, till sauce is fairly thick.
Serve with rice pilaf.

MINCE BALLS

Serves: 4
Electric frypan

750 g sausage meat
2 cups soft breadcrumbs
½ cup carrot, grated
salt and pepper
1 egg yolk
1 x 865 g (28 oz) can beef and vegetable
soup
2 tomatoes, skinned and chopped
½ onion, sliced

Combine meat, breadcrumbs, carrot, pepper and salt and
bind with egg yolk. Form mixture into 12 or 14 balls with
floured hands and place in electric frypan or a large
saucepan. Heat beef and vegetable soup, tomato and onion
and pour this sauce over meat balls. Place lid on frypan or
saucepan and simmer for 30-35 minutes. Serve with
buttered shell noodles or spaghetti, sprinkled lightly with
sesame or poppy seeds.

CURRIED LAMB CHOPS

Serves: 2-4
Electric frypan

4 lamb chump chops
seasoned meat tenderiser
2 tablespoons oil
1 teaspoon salt
2 teaspoons curry paste or curry powder
  (more if you like hot curries)
¼ teaspoon ground ginger or grated root
  ginger
1 teaspoon turmeric
1 onion, chopped
1 apple, peeled and sliced
2 cups water
1 cup rice
4 slices lemon

Pierce chops in a few places with a pointed knife. Sprinkle with tenderiser and rub in well. Heat oil in electric frypan add chops and brown well on all sides. Mix salt, curry paste or powder, ginger and turmeric, and spread over meat. Sprinkle onion and apple over the top. Pour in the water. Cover with lid and simmer gently for 30-45 minutes. Sprinkle in rice and lemon slices, cover and cook a further 30 minutes or till rice is cooked and meat is tender. You may need to add a bit of extra water near the end of cooking if curry becomes too dry. Serve with separate bowls of sliced bananas and cucumber chunks.

Note: Curried Lamb Chops may also be cooked in a lidded casserole dish in a moderately slow oven for 15-30 minutes or until tender.

The Entertainers

Casseroles seem to have been invented especially for parties. Not only can they be made days in advance, but, in fact, they're better that way, for it gives the flavours a chance to meld and mellow.

With a party coming up, you need an enormous casserole dish. But even if you have a huge dish, it can still be a problem fitting it into the oven. The answer is so simple — make your own casserole dish by using a plastic oven bag to hold in the juices. Then all you need is a large baking dish — the bigger the better when you have to cater for a hungry horde.

These recipes provide 12 or more servings. Most of them have been designed with oven bags in mind; but, they're also marvellous cooked in a lidded casserole dish or saucepan if you have one large enough to cope with the quantities.

To make entertaining even easier I've organised the recipes into five mix and match menus. If you cook up all three recipes on the menu you'll be able to serve between 30 and 40 people. If you've got half that number of guests, cook half the quantity of each recipe or use only two recipes.

MENU 1
Beef Burgundy
Veal Birds Tropicana
Chinese Chicken Wing

MENU 2
Lemon Chicken
Carbonnade of Beef
Paprika Pork Chops

MENU 3
Saucy Lamb Chops
Chicken Berlin
Lomo Con Jerez

MENU 4
German Pork
Chops in Cider
Sour Creamed Potatoes

MENU 5   A FLURRY OF CURRIES
Spice Islands Chicken
Curry in a Hurry
Cardamom and Sweet Potatoes (See page 102
   Use double quantities.)

OVEN BAG CASSEROLES

1 Sprinkle flour inside the oven bag. (This prevents the bag from bursting.) Place the bag in a baking dish.

2 Add casserole ingredients. This recipe is for Lemon Chicken. Tie the bag with a twist tie and puncture three or four holes in the top with a carving fork or skewer, just near the tie end, to allow the steam to escape.

3 Bake in a moderate oven for the required time. For Lemon Chicken it was 1 hour. Remove the casserole from the bag and arrange in the hot dish and there you have it — chicken in the bag!

BEEF BURGUNDY

Serves: 16
Oven temperature: moderate

1 large oven bag
2 kg (4 lb) chuck steak, cut into large
    cubes
1¼ cups button mushrooms
24 small onions
12 carrots, cut into small chunks
3-4 cloves garlic, crushed
½ cup plain flour
2-3 cups water
4 cups red burgundy (or claret)
2 teaspoons salt
pepper to season
2 teaspoons Parisian essence or gravy
    browning (otional)
4-6 beef stock cubes, crumbled

Arrange the oven bag in a shallow metal baking dish. Place meat, mushrooms, onions, carrots and garlic into bag or into a casserole dish. Combine the flour with the water, wine, salt, pepper, Parisian essence or gravy browning, and stock cubes and pour into bag or dish. Tie bag with twist tie and puncture 3 or 4 holes in top of bag with carving fork at tie end or cover casserole with lid. Bake in a moderate oven for 1½ hours. Serve with boiled potatoes in their jackets garnished with sour cream and chives, and small buttered brussels sprouts.

VEAL BIRDS TROPICANA

Serves: 12
Oven temperature: moderate

1 large oven bag
12 thin slices veal steak, as for schnitzel
1½ teaspoons salt
1¼ teaspoons pepper
12 bananas, cut into halves lengthwise
¾ cup plain flour
9 teaspoons curry powder
1½ cups white wine
1¼ teaspoons salt
6 teaspoons brown sugar
3 cups sour cream
3 chicken stock cubes, crumbled

Arrange the oven bag in a shallow metal baking dish. Cut each piece of veal in half and season with salt and pepper. Place a piece of banana in the centre of each piece of veal, roll up and secure with toothpicks. Place rolls in oven bag or in a casserole dish. Blend the flour and curry powder with the wine, add the remaining ingredients, and pour over the veal rolls. Tie bag with twist tie and puncture 3 or 4 holes in top of bag with carving fork at tie end or cover casserole with lid. Bake in a moderate oven for 45 minutes. Serve with fluffy boiled rice and fried pineapple rings.

CHINESE CHICKEN WINGS

Serves: 12
Oven temperature: moderate

2 kg (4 lb) chicken wings
1 oven bag, lightly floured
4 tablespoons soy sauce
2 tablespoons finely chopped ginger
1 tablespoon sugar
1 teaspoon pepper
4 tablespoons brandy
¼ cup chicken stock (see page 154)

Place the chicken wings carefully into the floured oven bag. Combine the soy sauce, ginger, sugar, pepper and brandy and chicken stock and pour over the wings. Tie bag with twist tie and allow the wings to marinate for at least 4 hours in the refrigerator. Arrange the oven bag in a shallow metal baking dish. Puncture 3 or 4 holes in top of bag with carving fork at tie end. Bake in a moderate oven for 1 hour or till tender. Serve with fried rice and braised celery.

Note: This recipe is especially suitable for buffet meals.

Chinese Chicken Wings may also be cooked in a large casserole dish, covered during cooking.

LEMON CHICKEN

Serves: 12-16
Oven temperature: moderate

1 large oven bag
4.5 kg (9 lb) chicken pieces
3 large lemons, thinly sliced
6 tablespoons cornflour
3 cups water
6 tablespoons brandy
6 teaspoons soy sauce
3 tablespoons sugar
1½ teaspoons salt
3 tablespoons finely chopped green
  ginger

Arrange the oven bag in a shallow metal baking dish. Place the chicken pieces and lemon slices in the bag or into a casserole dish. Combine the cornflour with the water, add the brandy, soy sauce, sugar, salt and ginger and pour over the chicken and lemon. Tie bag with twist tie and puncture 3 or 4 holes in top of bag with carving fork at tie end or cover casserole with lid. Bake in a moderate oven for 1 hour or till tender. Serve with fluffy boiled rice and mixed vegetables.

CARBONNADE OF BEEF

Serves: 12-16
Oven temperature: moderate

6 tablespoons plain flour
3 teaspoons salt
pinch of pepper, nutmeg and sugar
2.25 kg (4½ lb) stewing steak, cut into
  large chunks
1 large oven bag
6 medium onions, thinly sliced
3 cloves garlic, crushed
3 bouquet garni (see page 82) (optional)
3 cups hot water
3 cups beer
6 beef stock cubes, crumbled
3 teaspoons vinegar
3 tablespoons french mustard
thin slices french bread

Combine the flour, salt, pepper, nutmeg and sugar. Coat the meat with this mixture. Arrange the oven bag in a shallow metal baking dish. Place meat, onions, garlic and bouquet garni into bag or in a casserole dish. Combine water, beer, beef cubes, vinegar and half of the mustard and pour over the meat and vegetables. Tie bag with twist tie and puncture 3 or 4 holes in top of bag with carving fork at tie end or cover casserole with lid. Bake in a moderate oven for 1½ hours. Remove from oven and transfer contents of bag to a heated shallow ovenproof dish. Spread remaining mustard over bread and arrange slices over meat in dish or casserole. Place under a hot griller until bread is crisp. Serve with green beans and cauliflower in cheese sauce.

PAPRIKA PORK CHOPS

Serves: 12
Oven temperature: moderate

1 large oven bag
12 pork chops
1 teaspoon salt
¾ teaspoon pepper
3 teaspoons paprika
2¼ cups dry white wine
6 cloves garlic, crushed
pinch caraway seed (optional)
3 small onions, finely chopped
6 tablespoons finely chopped parsley
3 tablespoons brown sugar
6 teaspoons plain flour

Arrange floured oven bag in a shallow metal baking dish. Place chops evenly into base of bag or into a wide casserole dish. Combine all ingredients and pour over the chops. Tie bag with twist tie or cover casserole with lid and allow chops to marinate for 2 hours. Puncture 3 or 4 holes in top of bag with carving fork at tie end before cooking. Bake in a moderate oven for 50-60 minutes. Serve with pasta and fresh broccoli.

SAUCY LAMB CHOPS

Serves: 12-16
Oven temperature: moderate

1 large oven bag
12-16 large lamb chump chops
6 cloves garlic, crushed
6 onions, finely chopped
6 beef stock cubes, crumbled
3 cans condensed tomato soup (about 425 g or 15 oz cans)
3 cups red wine or water
¾ cup tomato paste
3 tablespoons chopped parsley
6 rashers bacon, chopped
3 teaspoons dry mustard
6 tablespoons plain flour
3 tablespoons Worcestershire sauce

Arrange the oven bag in a shallow metal baking dish. Place lamb chops in bag or casserole dish. Combine all remaining ingredients and mix well. Pour over the chops. If using a casserole dish, cover with a lid. If using oven bag, tie bag with twist tie and puncture 3 or 4 holes in top of bag with carving fork at tie end. Bake in moderate oven for 1½ hours or till tender. Serve with cauliflower, peas and boiled rice.

CHICKEN BERLIN

Serves: 10-12
Oven temperature: moderate

1 x 3 kg (6 lb) chicken
1 tablespoon butter or margarine
1 tablespoon oil
1 large oven bag
2 large cans condensed vegetable soup (about 830 g or 30 oz)
1 cup beer
½ cup chopped parsley
freshly ground pepper

Remove skin from chicken and cut into pieces (see page 46). Melt butter or margarine and oil in a frying pan and cook chicken pieces until golden brown. Remove chicken and place in an oven bag and place oven bag in shallow oven dish. Put soup, beer, parsley and pepper in a bowl and mix thoroughly. Pour this mixture over the chicken pieces. Tie bag with twist tie and puncture with 3 or 4 holes at tie end. Cover and cook in a moderate oven until chicken is tender, 1-1½ hours. Serve with fluffy rice or buttered whole potatoes and a green salad. For an extra elegant touch sprinkle potatoes with toasted sesame seeds.

Note: Chicken Berlin can also be cooked in a large casserole dish, covered during the cooking time.

LOMO CON JEREZ

Serves: 12-16
Oven temperature: moderately hot lowering to moderate

1 x 2.5-3 kg (5-6 lb) loin of pork
2½ teaspoons salt
½ teaspoon freshly ground black pepper
½ teaspoon ground cummin
½ teaspoon powdered saffron
2 cloves garlic, crushed
2 tablespoons finely chopped parsley
2 tablespoons olive oil
2 cups medium dry sherry

Ask the butcher to trim fat and tie the loin. Rub with a mixture of the salt, pepper, cummin, saffron, garlic and parsley. Let stand for 2 hours.

Heat oil in a deep roasting pan or Dutch oven. Brown the pork in it on all sides, then roast in a hot oven for 30 minutes. Pour off fat and add sherry. Top with a lid and continue to cook in a moderate oven for a further 1¾ hours basting frequently or until pork is tender and well done. Serve hot with saffron rice.

GERMAN PORK

Serves: 10-12
Oven temperature: moderate

Marinade
1½ cups red wine
4 tablespoons wine vinegar
1 white onion, finely chopped
1 carrot, diced
grated rind of 1 lemon
2 bay leaves, coarsely crushed
**1 teaspoon fresh tarragon or a pinch of
   dried tarragon**
¼ teaspoon ground cloves
¼ teaspoon ground allspice
¼ teaspoon ground ginger
1 teaspoon black pepper
12 juniper berries
1 teaspoon salt

Pork
**1 x 2.5 kg (5 lb) leg of pork, approximate
   weight**
1 tablespoon oil
1 cup stock, or water and stock cube
cornflour to thicken

To prepare marinade: Place all ingredients into a very large glass, pottery or plastic mixing bowl. Crush the juniper berries lightly when you add them, using either a mortar and pestle or a rolling pin. Place the pork in the mixture, making sure the bowl is large enough to hold it comfortably. Cover with foil. Marinate for several days, turning once or twice a day. When you want to cook the pork remove it from the marinade and dry thoroughly with kitchen paper. Brush away any vegetables or herbs sticking to the outside.

To prepare pork: Heat the oil in a pan and then add the pork, browning well on all sides while turning frequently. Remove. Strain the marinade into a bowl, pressing down hard on the vegetables before discarding them. Mix the strained marinade with the stock, or water and stock cubes, and add this to the pan in which you browned the pork. Bring the liquid to the boil, scraping any brown bits on the base of the pan into the juices.

Place the pork in a large casserole dish, pour over the marinade mixture and cover the casserole with a lid. Bake in a moderate oven for about 2 hours or until the pork is tender, basting every half hour. When cooked transfer the pork to a heated dish, cover and leave it aside in a warm place for about 15 minutes for easier carving.

Pour the cooking liquid into a saucepan. If it seems too fatty, skim away as much fat as possible. Mix together a little cornflour and water to make a cream and add to the sauce until it is the consistency of very thin cream. Check for seasoning and leave the sauce to cook gently for about 5 minutes. Carve the pork thinly and arrange on a heated platter, serving the sauce separately.

Note: This pork is also marvellous served cold.

CHOPS IN CIDER

Serves: 12
Oven temperature: moderate

1 large oven bag
12 forequarter lamb chops
3 medium onions, finely chopped
3 cloves garlic, crushed
6 tablespoons tomato ketchup
1½ cups apple cider
6 teaspoons soy sauce
6 tablespoons chutney
3 tablespoons brown sugar
3 teaspoons salt
¾ teaspoon pepper
3 tablespoons plain flour

Arrange the oven bag in a shallow metal baking dish. Place chops in bag or in a casserole dish. Combine remaining ingredients and pour over chops. Tie bag with twist tie and puncture 3 or 4 holes in top of bag with carving fork at tie end or cover casserole. Bake in a moderate oven for 45 minutes. Serve with potatoes and vegetables in season.

Front left: Chicken with Olives (page 148);
front right: Beef Burgundy (page 139)

LAPIN PIE

Serves: 12-16
Oven temperature: moderately slow,
then raise to hot

3 rabbits or 3 x 1.5 kg (3 lb) chickens
2 cups red wine
3 cloves garlic, crushed
185 g (6 oz) bacon pieces
8 baby onions, or 3 medium onions
1 cup apricot juice
2 chicken stock cubes
1 teaspoon dried or fresh thyme
salt and pepper
1 cup dried apricots
1 cup prunes
3 tablespoons plain flour
3 tablespoons butter or margarine
500 g (16 oz) frozen puff pastry
1 beaten egg for glazing

Cut rabbits or chickens into joints. (See page 46 for chickens). If using rabbits, chop off legs and chop back into pieces, giving 6-8 joints in all. Place rabbit or chicken in a bowl with red wine and garlic and leave to soak for a few hours, or overnight if possible. Trim rind off bacon pieces and place in a large frying pan. Fry until bacon is browned and fat is starting to run. Remove. Add drained rabbit or chicken pieces to pan and fry till well browned. Remove. Trim baby onions or quarter large onions and brown in pan, then add apricot nectar and scrape up all the crusty bits on the bottom.

Place rabbit or chicken, bacon, onion and pan juices in a large saucepan. Add wine and garlic mixture, stock cubes, thyme, salt, pepper, dried apricots and prunes (with stones removed if preferred). Top with a lid and gently simmer till meat is tender, about 1½ hours (or pressure cook for about ½ an hour). Lapin Pie can also be cooked in a lidded casserole dish in a moderately slow oven for 1-1½ hours or until tender.

Mix flour with butter or margarine to form a stiff paste. Add small blobs of this mixture to the juices in the pan and stir over a low heat until liquid boils. Add more blobs of butter/flour mixture until the liquid is thick enough. Cool. This can all be done in advance. The pie can even be assembled including the pastry topping beforehand with just the final cooking done at the serving time.

Place rabbit or chicken into a pie dish, piling the pieces up in the centre. Instead of a deep pie dish I use my large ovenproof Lieki baking dish. It only has an edge 5 cm (2 inches) high. The large, shallow pie means everyone receives a decent piece of pastry. Arrange prunes and apricots evenly throughout mixture so each serving has some. Spoon the sauce over the meat and fruit. Roll out pastry very thinly. Trim off a thin strip long enough to fit around the pie dish edge. Brush pastry strip with egg or water and place rolled out pastry over pie, pressing edges together well. Brush top with beaten egg and make a hole in the centre. Bake in a hot oven for 25-30 minutes or until pastry is cooked and golden brown.

From back to front: Sunshine Dumplings (page 156);
Filo Pastry (page 150);
Mashed Potato (page 152);
Courgette and Tomato Topping (page 153)

SOUR-CREAMED POTATOES

Serves: 12
Oven temperature: moderate

1 large oven bag
2 kg (4 lb) small new potatoes
12 spring onions, finely sliced
2 cups sour cream
1 teaspoon salt
½ teaspoon pepper
2 teaspoons finely grated lemon rind
pinch nutmeg

Arrange the oven bag in a large baking dish. Wash and dry the potatoes and place in oven bag or in a large baking dish. Combine the spring onions, sour cream, salt, pepper, lemon rind and nutmeg and pour over the potatoes. Tie bag with twist tie and puncture 3 or 4 holes in top of bag with a carving fork at tie end or cover baking dish with foil or lid. Bake in a moderate oven for 1½-2 hours, or till tender. Serve with veal dishes.

If you haven't got a large enough baking dish, halve the quantity and cook in 2 lots. This takes slightly less time.

Variation: If new potatoes are not in season use 1 kg (2 lb) thickly sliced, peeled potatoes. Arrange in a shallow layer, no deeper than 5 cm (2 inches) in dish and continue recipe normally.

SPICE ISLANDS CHICKEN

Serves: 12
Oven temperature: moderate

1 large oven bag
12 medium chicken breasts
3 tablespoons plain flour
3 cups water
3 tablespoons butter or margarine
1 teaspoon salt, or to taste
ground black pepper
3 teaspoons turmeric
1¼ teaspoons cummin
pinch chilli powder
1¼ teaspoons ground ginger
3 teaspoons curry powder
3 chicken stock cubes, crumbled
6 tablespoons onion flakes

Arrange the oven bag in a shallow metal baking dish and add the chicken breasts or put them into a casserole dish. Combine the flour and water, add the remaining ingredients and pour over the chicken. Tie bag with twist tie and puncture 3 or 4 holes in top of bag with carving fork at tie end, or cover casserole with lid. Bake in a moderate oven for about 1 hour. Serve with fluffy boiled rice, papadoms and curry accompaniments.

Note: This recipe is particularly suitable for buffet entertaining.

CURRY IN A HURRY

Serves: 12
Oven temperature: moderate

1 large oven bag
6 cups frozen prawns, thawed and dried
3 bananas, peeled and sliced
3 apples, chopped
3 onions, finely chopped
¾ cup plain flour
3 tablespoons curry powder, more if
  desired
6 cups water
6 chicken stock cubes, crumbled
3 tablespoons lemon juice
pinch salt

Arrange the oven bag in a shallow metal baking dish. Place the prawns, bananas, apples and onions in the bag or in a casserole dish. Combine the flour and curry powder with water, add the stock cubes, lemon juice and salt. Spoon or pour over the prawns in the bag or in the dish. Tie bag with twist tie and puncture 3 or 4 holes in top of bag with carving fork at tie end or cover casserole with lid. Bake in a moderate oven for 20 minutes. Serve with fluffy boiled rice.

BRAISED FILLET OF BEEF

Serves: 8-10
Oven temperature: moderate

**1 trimmed fillet of beef, approximate
  weight 2 kg (4 lb)**

Stuffing
125 g (4 oz) liver pâté or pâté de foie gras
2 tablespoons chopped spring onions
1 tablespoon butter
1 tablespoon Madeira
½ tablespoon brandy
pinch allspice, thyme and pepper

Braising
½ cup carrots, chopped
½ cup celery, chopped
½ cup onions, chopped
½ cup ham, diced
4 tablespoons butter or margarine
sprig parsley
pinch thyme
½ cup Madeira
1 tablespoon oil
**1 cup beef consommé, or water and beef
  stock cubes**
cornflour

This is a no-expense spared dish which makes a
magnificent meal for that extra-special dinner party. It's
not very complicated and most of the preparation can be
done the day before.

To prepare stuffing: Cut a deep long pocket down the
length of the fillet. Mix the pâté with all other stuffing
ingredients and stir well to combine. Spread this mixture
inside the pocket in the beef. Tie up the beef neatly with
white string (it doesn't flavour the meat) at short
intervals.

To prepare braised fillet: Gently fry the carrots, onions,
celery and ham in 2 tablespoons of the butter or
margarine till softened but not brown. Add the parsley,
thyme and Madeira and boil until it is almost absorbed
by the vegetables. Tip onto a plate.

Melt the remaining butter or margarine and oil in the pan
and fry the fillet on all sides. Place in a casserole dish.
Spread carrot mixture over the beef and pour consommé
or water and stock cubes into the dish. All these
preparations can be done beforehand.

Top with a lid and bake in a moderate oven for 40-55
minutes, basting a few times during the cooking. (I use a
meat thermometer to ensure the beef is not overcooked.)
When done, place beef on a serving plate and remove
string. Stand for 10 minutes. Make the sauce by boiling
the cooking liquid rapidly until reduced by half. Thicken
with a little cornflour mixed to a cream with cold water.
Add just enough to make a thin sauce. Spoon a little
sauce over the beef to glaze and serve the rest in a
separate sauce boat.

PORK GINGER MEGGS

Serves: 10-12
Oven temperature: moderate

½ cup soy sauce
1 cup sweet cider
36 pieces pork spareribs, well trimmed
3 tablespoons oil
3 tablespoons butter or margarine
salt and pepper
1 large piece fresh ginger root
**1 cup chicken stock (see page 154) or
  water and stock cube**
**2 teaspoons potato flour, or cornflour,
  mixed with a little cold water**
chopped parsley

Mix together the soy sauce and cider in an enamel or
glass dish. Add pork, stir and leave to soak for 1 hour,
turning occasionally. Drain, heat oil and butter or
margarine and brown spareribs lightly for a few minutes
on each side. Fry in 2 or 3 batches. Add extra oil and
butter if required. Place meat in a flat baking dish, season
with salt and pepper. Slice ginger root very thinly and
scatter over the pork. Pour remaining marinade over
meat and bake in a moderate oven for 50-60 minutes,
turning meat once or twice and adding a little chicken
stock as necessary to keep meat from drying out. When
meat is cooked combine potato flour or cornflour and
water mixture with the remaining stock and pour over
the meat. Stir well then return pan to oven for 5 minutes
until sauce thickens slightly. Sprinkle with parsley and
serve with fried potato and apple slices.

BEEF POT ROAST

Serves: 8-10
Oven temperature: slow

**1.5-2 kg (3-4 lb) pot roast, rolled chuck
  or brisket of beef**
**plain flour seasoned with salt and
  pepper**
2 tablespoons dripping
1 onion, chopped
2 carrots, chopped
3 stalks celery, chopped
2 turnips, chopped
1 whole onion studded with cloves
**2 cups beef stock (see page 154) or water
  with beef stock cubes**
salt and pepper

Trim the meat if necessary and tie into a neat shape with white string. It is easiest to ask your butcher to do this for you. Roll the meat in a few tablespoons of flour mixed with salt and pepper. Heat the dripping in a deep saucepan and brown the meat all over, on a high heat. When you are browning the last side add the chopped vegetables and fry until they start to soften. Add the whole onion, then pour in the stock or water and stock cubes, and add salt and pepper to taste. Cover and either cook very gently on top of the stove, or in a slow oven for 2-3 hours, until tender. Turn the meat a few times during the cooking and skim off any excess fat. When the meat is tender, remove it to a serving plate. Boil the liquid in the pot over a high heat until it forms a thick sauce. Serve the sauce with the vegetables or strain it and serve in a sauceboat. This goes well with boiled potatoes tossed in butter and poppyseeds.

CHICKEN WITH OLIVES

Serves: 8-12
Oven temperature: moderate

**2 x 2 kg (4 lb) chickens or 4 kg (6 lb) of
  chicken pieces**
4 tablespoons butter or margarine
4 tablespoons oil
6 sticks celery, chopped
1 cup chopped spring onions
1 kg (2 lb) courgettes, sliced
2-4 cloves garlic, crushed (optional)
¼ cup plain flour
**1 teaspoon dried marjoram or 2
  teaspoons freshly chopped
  marjoram**
2 cups white wine
**2 cups chicken stock (see page 154) or
  water and 2-3 chicken stock cubes**
1 cup olives, black and/or stuffed
salt and pepper
½ cup double cream

Cut chicken into joints (see page 46). Fry in butter or margarine and oil till well browned. Remove from pan and place in a casserole dish. Add celery, spring onions, courgettes and garlic to pan and sprinkle with flour and herbs and cook for a few minutes till flour and vegetables start to turn golden brown. Off the heat, add wine and stock, or water and stock cubes and stir till well combined. Bring to the boil and simmer a few minutes, scraping up the crusty bits and pieces in the pan. Pour over chicken. Add olives. Top with a lid and cook in a moderate oven for 1-1½ hours or till tender. Taste, and add salt and pepper if necessary. Just before serving add cream and stir well to mix.

Topping it off

They say you can't judge a book by its cover, but presentation sure can make a big difference in cooking. Cover a casserole with a delicious topping and you can turn a homely stew into a dinner party dish.

A crisp, buttery layer of puff pastry, with a crunch in every bite, makes any casserole special. Serve your casserole with puffed and golden dumplings; this will make a mouth-watering dinner. Or, add a splash of colour with courgettes and tomato slices, before you take the dish to the table. These are just a few ideas for making a special casserole when your invitation says 'formal'.

TRIMMINGS AND TOPPINGS PASTRY

1 *Puff pastry.* It's best if the casserole is allowed to get cold before topping with pastry. Just roll out thawed frozen puff pastry thinly, until it is large enough to cover the casserole dish. Cut a strip of pastry long enough to fit around the edge of the casserole dish. Brush the casserole edge with water, then lay the pastry strip around the edge, pressing it down gently, and brush it with water. Cover the whole with the rolled out pastry piece and press the edges firmly together. Trim off the excess pastry with a knife. Decorate the edge by pinching with your fingers, or pressing with a fork. Make a hole in the centre and brush pastry with beaten egg. Decorate with pastry roses and leaves made from the pastry trimmings if you wish. Bake in a hot oven for 20-25 minutes, or until the pastry is puffed and cooked.

2 *Filo pastry.* This wafer thin pastry is available ready made from cake shops or delicatessens, particularly in a Greek area of town. Cool the casserole before topping with this pastry.

Brush the casserole edge with water then place a layer of pastry over the dish. Brush this layer with melted butter or margarine, then top with a second layer of pastry. Repeat layers of pastry, brushing each one with melted butter, until there are 8 layers in all. Trim the edges. Bake in a hot oven for 20 minutes or until pastry is crisp and golden brown.

3 *Pastry rounds.* Roll out bought puff pastry or flaky pastry thinly and cut into rounds with a biscuit or cookie cutter. Place on a greased cookie tray and bake in a hot oven for 10-15 minutes or until puffed, golden brown and dry. Arrange these rounds over the top of the hot, cooked casserole.

4 *Pastry crescents.* Roll out bought puff pastry thinly and cut into crescent shapes with a round biscuit cutter. Place on a greased cookie tray and bake in a hot oven for 7-10 minutes or until golden brown. Arrange the crescents over the hot casserole.

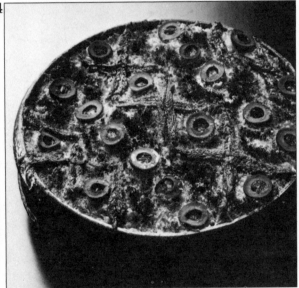

BREAD TOPPINGS

1 *French rounds.* Cut a French loaf into thin slices. Brush each slice with melted butter or margarine and place on top of the cooked casserole. Bake in a hot oven for 10 minutes, or until bread is crisp and golden brown. The melted butter or margarine may be flavoured with crushed garlic if you like.

2 *Cheesey rounds.* Cut sliced bread into rounds with a biscuit cutter and arrange in overlapping layers on top of a hot, cooked casserole. Sprinkle the rounds with finely grated cheddar cheese. Bake in a hot oven until cheese is melted and topping is golden brown.

3 *Crumb topping.* Mix together equal quantities of grated cheese and dry breadcrumbs, using about ¼ cup of each. Sprinkle this mixture over the top of the cooked casserole, then sprinkle with paprika. Brown in a hot oven for about 10 minutes.

4 *Anchovy topping.* Sprinkle the cooked casserole with a mixture of equal quantities of grated cheese and breadcrumbs. Top with strips of anchovy fillets and decorate with sliced stuffed olives. Brown in a hot oven for about 10 minutes.

DUMPLINGS AND POTATOES

1 *Dumplings.* Drop spoonfuls of soft dumpling mixture on top of the simmering casserole 20 minutes before the end of the cooking time. Cover with a lid and finish cooking on top of the stove. If cooking the casserole in the oven leave the lid off for crisper dumplings. (See page 156 for dumpling recipe.)

2 *Mashed swirled potato.* Make up mashed potatoes, mixing with lashings of butter, milk or cream. Spoon over the top of the cooked casserole and swirl surface, then sprinkle with grated cheese, sesame seeds or poppy seeds. If you like brush with beaten egg before sprinkling. Brown in a hot oven.

Grated cheese can also be mixed into the hot mashed potato. Use freshly cooked mashed potato, or make up a packet of instant potatoes.

3 *Piped potatoes.* Use a piping bag with a fluted nozzle to pipe potato on top of a basic casserole for a luxury look. I like to use instant mashed potatoes for piping as there's no chance of lumps catching in the nozzle. Brown the potato topping in a hot oven.

4 *Sliced potato topping.* Slice cooked potatoes thinly and arrange them in overlapping layers over the top of a cooked casserole. Brown the slices in a hot oven. For a speedy topping use canned baby potatoes.

PASTA TOPPINGS

1 *Macaroni shells.* Cook macaroni shells or shapes till tender in boiling salted water. Drain well and toss in butter or margarine. Pile on top of cooked casserole. Sprinkle with grated cheese and place in a hot oven until cheese is brown.

2 *Ribbon macaroni or spaghetti.* Cook macaroni or spaghetti. Drain well and toss with butter or margarine and a handful of grated cheese if desired. Arrange the pasta around the outside edge of the hot casserole. If desired, sprinkle pasta with sesame or poppy seeds. Serve immediately.

3 *Rice Ring.* Cook rice in boiling salted water until tender. Drain well and press firmly into an oiled ring tin. Place the serving plate over the tin, turn the tin over and remove carefully so the rice ring slips out onto the plate. Fill the centre carefully with the hot casserole mixture.

VEGETABLE TOPPING

1 Decorate the top of the casserole with thin slices of courgette and tomato. Sprinkle with grated cheese and place in a moderate oven for 15-20 minutes, or until the cheese is golden and the vegetables have softened. Use any vegetables you like for topping — carrots, cucumber, peppers or onion rings are good. If desired, vegetables may be partially cooked in boiling water for a few minutes.

FISH STOCK

Makes approximately 5 cups

2 tablespoons butter, margarine or oil
1½ cups chopped soup vegetables
  (carrots, celery and onion)
scraps from fish, and shellfish heads and
  shells, plus any extra fish heads you
  can get from the fishmonger
juice of 1 lemon
3 cups water
1½ cups white wine
salt and pepper
2 bay leaves
1 teaspoon dried or fresh marjoram

Heat oil, butter or margarine and fry soup vegetables until softened. Add all other ingredients and bring to the boil. Simmer for 20-30 minutes. Strain and use as a base for fish soup.

CHICKEN STOCK

Makes approximately 4 cups

1 carrot
4 tough celery stalks
bones and carcass of 1 chicken, cooked
  or uncooked
1 onion, stuck with 4 whole cloves
strip lemon rind
1 teaspoon salt
6 peppercorns
3 cups water
1 cup white wine or extra cup water
¼ cup white vinegar

Chop vegetables roughly and break up bones and carcass as much as possible. Place all ingredients in a saucepan. Cover and bring slowly to the boil. Simmer for about 1 hour, or pressure cook for 20-30 minutes. Strain and skim off fat before using.

BEEF OR VEAL STOCK

Makes approximately 4 cups

1 kg (2 lb) cracked beef or veal bones
other ingredients as for chicken stock

Brown bones in a baking dish in a hot oven. Then follow chicken stock recipe substituting beef or veal bones for chicken bones.

SCONE TOPPINGS FOR CASSEROLES

Sufficient for one casserole
Oven temperature: hot

1 cup self raising flour
1 tablespoon instant full cream
  powdered milk
pinch salt
30 g (1 oz) butter or margarine
⅓ cup of water, approximately

Sift flour, powdered milk and salt together. Rub in butter or margarine. Add sufficient water to make a soft dough. Knead well then pat out on a floured board to about 2 cm (¾ inch) thick. Cut with a scone cutter. Place scones into a bubbling casserole (make sure it is actually bubbling). Raise the oven temperature to hot and replace casserole in the oven until scones are puffed and cooked.

154

EGG AND POTATO PIE

Serves: 4-5
Oven temperature: moderately hot

3 cups sliced cooked potato
3 hard-boiled eggs, sliced
2-3 rashers bacon, chopped
2 tablespoons cheese, finely grated
3-4 tablespoons butter or margarine
1½ tablespoons plain flour
½ teaspoon mustard
½ teaspoon salt
½ teaspoon celery salt
1½ cups milk
2 tablespoons butter and 1 cup soft
    breadcrumbs for topping

Prepare potato, eggs, bacon and cheese. Melt butter or margarine in a saucepan, add flour, mustard, salt and celery salt and mix well. Add milk in three portions, boiling and stirring between additions. Place half the sliced potato in a greased ovenproof dish. Add half the eggs, bacon and cheese and cover with half the sauce. Repeat with remaining ingredients.

To make buttered crumbs for topping, melt the butter or margarine, remove from heat and toss the crumbs in it. Sprinkle over the pie. Bake uncovered in a moderately hot oven for 30-45 minutes, depending on the shape of the dish (longer if it is a deep dish). Serve hot.

Variation: Bacon may be cooked first if desired and the bacon fat used with the butter in the sauce. Fresh or dried herbs can be added for extra flavour.

FAVOURITE MEAT PIE

Serves: 6-8
Oven temperature: moderately hot

1 kg (2 lb) chuck or skirt steak
2 tablespoons oil
2 onions, chopped
½ cup celery, chopped
½ cup carrot, chopped
2 cups beef stock (see page 154) or water
    and beef stock cubes
2 teaspoons salt
¼ teaspoon black or freshly ground
    pepper
¼ teaspoon ground nutmeg
1 teaspoon meat extract
3 tablespoons plain flour
185 g (6 oz) wholemeal pastry (see
    page 156)
beaten egg for glazing

Cut steak into cubes. Heat oil in a large saucepan, fry steak in about 3 lots until browned, remove. Fry onion until browned, add celery and carrot and cook a few minutes. Replace meat, add stock, salt, pepper and nutmeg, cover, and simmer gently for 2 hours, or until cooked, or transfer contents of saucepan to a casserole dish and cook, covered, in a moderately slow oven for 1½-2 hours, or until tender. Blend meat extract and flour to a smooth paste with a little cold water, add to saucepan, and allow sauce to thicken. Taste and adjust seasoning if necessary.

Put meat in a 1½-2 pint pie dish, place a pie funnel in centre, add sufficient gravy to come within 2.5 cm (1 inch) of top and reserve remainder for serving. Make pastry, and roll out on a lightly floured board until 2.5 cm (1 inch) larger than top of dish. Cut a strip about 1 cm (½ inch) wide, place on edge of dish which has been previously glazed with water, press down, then brush strip of pastry with water. Lift remaining pastry onto pie, easing it gently. (If stretched it will shrink in cooking.) Press edges together, trim and decorate with a knife. Glaze pastry with beaten egg. Roll out any pastry scraps, make a rose and leaves and place on pie around hole for funnel. With a knife or skewer, make a few extra holes in pastry for steam to escape. Bake in a moderately hot oven for 25 minutes or until cooked.

Variation: Add 2 lambs' kidneys or ½ an ox kidney to steak. Wash well, trim, skin and chop into small pieces, before adding.

SUNSHINE DUMPLINGS

Makes 6 dumplings
Oven temperature: hot

1 cup self raising flour
½ cup instant full cream powdered milk
½ teaspoon salt
30 g (1 oz) butter or margarine
½ cup water

Sift the dry ingredients. Rub in the butter or margarine until the mixture resembles breadcrumbs. Add water and mix well with a wooden spoon. Drop heaped tablespoons of dumpling mixture into a bubbling casserole. If it's on top of the stove, cover with a lid, or bake, uncovered, in a hot oven for 20 minutes or until dumplings are cooked and golden.

Variation: Add 2 tablespoons poppy seeds, 2 tablespoons chopped parsley, 2 tablespoons sesame seeds, or 3 tablespoons grated cheese to the basic mixture.

WHOLEMEAL PASTRY

Sufficient to cover one casserole
Oven temperature: hot

1 cup All Bran cereal
½ cup water
1½ cups wholemeal self raising flour
½ cup instant full cream powdered milk
pinch salt
125 g (4 oz) butter or margarine

Soak All Bran in water until liquid is absorbed, approximately 5 minutes. Sift flour, powdered milk and salt together. Rub in butter or margarine until ingredients resemble breadcrumbs. Add bran mixture and knead till smooth. Roll out thinly and use to top a casserole. Cook in a hot oven for 20-25 minutes, or until brown and cooked.

PORK CASSEROLE WITH HERB SCONE TOP

Serves: 6-8
Oven temperature: slow;
hot to cook topping

Filling
1 kg (2 lb) lean pork
2 tablespoons fine, wholemeal flour
salt and pepper
1 onion, chopped
2 cloves garlic, chopped
60 g (2 oz) preserved ginger
6 prunes, stoned
1 bouquet garni (a bay leaf, a sprig each
  of marjoram, parsley and thyme tied
  together) or 2 teaspoons dried bouquet
  garni
1 cup red wine

Herb Scone Top
90 g (3 oz) butter or margarine
185 g (6 oz) fine wholemeal self raising
  flour
pinch salt
2 tablespoons chopped parsley
cold water to mix

To prepare filling: Trim pork and dice then roll in flour, salt and pepper. Place in a casserole in alternate layers with other ingredients, adding the wine last. Put lid on and cook in slow oven for 2 hours. Remove lid, take out bouquet garni if using fresh herbs, place herb scone dough on top, turn heat up to hot and leave to cook a further 10-15 minutes until topping is brown. Serve hot.

To prepare Herb Scone Top: Rub butter or margarine into flour and salt, add parsley, stir in enough cold water to make a fairly stiff dough. Roll out lightly on a floured surface, lift carefully onto bubbling casserole and mark into squares with a sharp knife.

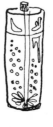

STEAK AND KIDNEY PIE

Serves: 4-6
Oven temperature: moderately slow;
raise to hot

500 g (1 lb) chuck steak
125 g (4 oz) ox or lamb's kidney
2 tablespoons dripping or oil
2 onions, chopped
3 tablespoons plain flour
2½ cups water, or beef stock made with
beef stock cubes
salt and pepper
250 g (8 oz) flaky, puff or shortcrust
pastry
1 egg yolk, beaten with a little water, for
glazing

Remove gristle and fat from meat and cut into cubes. Skin and core kidney and cut into small pieces. Fry steak in hot dripping or oil in a heavy saucepan until lightly browned. Add kidneys, onion and flour and cook gently for 5 minutes. Add water, salt and pepper and bring to the boil stirring continuously. Reduce heat and simmer, covered, until steak and kidney are tender, about 1½-2 hours. Or transfer into a casserole dish and bake in a moderately slow oven for 1½-2 hours or until tender. Place in a pie dish and allow to cool.

Roll out pastry on a lightly floured board until 2.5 cm (1 inch) larger than the top of pie dish or casserole. Cut to fit dish and cut remaining pastry into a strip 2.5 cm (1 inch) wide. Place strip on rim of dish, previously brushed with cold water. Brush pastry rim with cold water and cover with pastry top. Seal edges by pressing together, trim and decorate edge with fork or by pinching into scallop pattern. Cut a vent to allow stem to escape and decorate with a pastry rose and leaves made from any scraps. Brush pastry with egg glaze and bake in a hot oven for 20-30 minutes. Cover rose with aluminium foil if necessary to prevent burning. Serve hot.

COCONUT MILK

3 cups desiccated coconut
6 cups water

Put desiccated coconut into a saucepan, pour 3 cups of the water over and bring slowly to the boil. Allow to cool to lukewarm. Put into a liquidizer and blend at high speed for 2-3 minutes. Strain. If no liquidizer is available, knead coconut well when cool enough to handle and then strain through a fine strainer, pressing well to extract as much milk as possible. This is the first extract or thick milk. Repeat process with same coconut and 3 more cups water. This will give thinner milk, but it will still have good flavour.

BEURRE MANIÉ

2 tablespoons butter or margarine
2 tablespoons plain flour

Beat butter or margarine and flour together. Stir small pieces gradually into cooked stews and casseroles until thickened as desired.

INDEX